Creative BEDROOM DECORATING

Cover pictures: (tl) Classic canopy kit by Pavilion
Textiles, England. Tel: 01604 26901; (tr) IPC
Magazines/Robert Harding Syndication;
(b) Quilting by Sanderson, 6 Cavendish Square,
London W1M 0NE, England. Tel: 0171 636 7800.

Pages 1, 3: IPC Magazines/Robert Harding
Syndication; Page 4: Jane Churchill

Based on *Creating Your Home*, published in the UK
© Eaglemoss Publications Ltd 1995

First published in the USA in 1995
by Betterway Books,
an imprint of F&W Publications Inc.,
1507 Dana Avenue,
Cincinnati, Ohio 45207.

ISBN 1-55870-402-7

Manufactured in Hong Kong

10 9 8 7 6 5 4 3 2 1

Creative
BEDROOM
DECORATING

BETTERWAY BOOKS

Contents

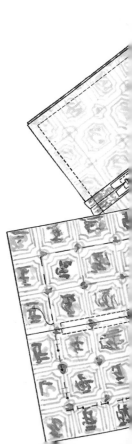

WINDOW TREATMENTS

CUSHIONS AND ACCESSORIES

INDEX   *127*

FITTED BEDSPREADS

*You can make a fitted bedspread to suit almost any type
of bed and room style. Cut to cover the bedclothes and bedbase
neatly, it gives a finished look to a bedroom.*

An attractive fitted bedspread completes the coordinated look of your bedroom. It's also a real asset in a guest bedroom or spare room if you don't have a second set of bedlinen – on wash days, you can just cover the mattress with the bedspread to restore the bed to its smart, made-up look. Alternatively, a fitted bedspread made for a divan creates a piece of chic and adaptable living room furniture that quickly converts to a bed when needed.

These instructions are for two bedspread designs. The gusseted bedspread has a skirt that goes all round the bed, with splits to accommodate the legs of a headboard and footboard. The skirt of the more traditional frilled bedspread covers the sides and foot of the bed and is made in one continuous length to fit a bed without a footboard. You can easily adapt either style to suit any type of bed by omitting or adding the splits in the skirt.

A piped trim, stitched between the main fabric panels, adds tailored definition to the bedspread. Use offcuts of the main fabric to make the piping or, for extra definition, choose a complementary plain or patterned fabric that picks up on one of the colours in the bedspread fabric.

To complete a fully-tailored look, line the bedspread in an inexpensive fabric, such as calico. The lining adds body to the top of the bedspread and improves the hang of the skirt.

A refreshing springtime print is shown to full effect on a fitted bedspread, where a generous expanse of fabric lies flat across the top of the bed and a lined skirt is gathered around the sides.

MAKING A GUSSETED BEDSPREAD

For your bedspread, choose a firmly woven, mediumweight fabric that is easy to work with and effectively hides the bedbase and bedclothes underneath. If the fabric has a directional design, take this into account when cutting out the bedspread pieces. For a bed with a head and footboard, make the skirt frill in separate sections to fit around the legs; otherwise, stitch the frill into one continuous strip. Cut the skirt to whatever length you prefer; you may wish to conceal the bedbase and legs completely, or make a shorter skirt to reveal attractive bedstead legs.

YOU WILL NEED

❖ FABRIC
❖ PIPING FABRIC
❖ PIPING CORD
❖ MATCHING SEWING THREAD
❖ TAPE MEASURE
❖ TAILORS' CHALK
❖ SCISSORS
❖ PINS

▶ For more information on making and adding piping see pages 11-12.

▣ *This short-skirted bedspread makes a lighthearted and chic daybed cover. Corner splits in the frill allow it to fit neatly around the bed legs.*

CUTTING THE FABRIC

1 Cutting the central panel Measure the length (**A**) and width (**B**) of the mattress, adding 3cm (1¼in) to each measurement for seam allowances. Cut and join fabric widths to make up a rectangle this size; if joining widths, centre a full width and join additional fabric widths to either side, matching any pattern across seams and taking 1.5cm (⅝in) seam allowances.

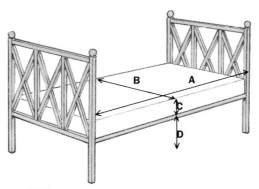

2 Cutting out the gusset Measure the depth of the mattress (**C**). Adding 3cm (1¼in) to each measurement for seam allowances, cut and join fabric widths to make two gusset side panels measuring **A** x **C**, and two gusset end panels measuring **B** x **C**; match any pattern across the seams when joining fabric widths.

3 Cutting out the frill Measure the frill width from the top of the bed base to the desired drop (**D**) plus 3.5cm (1⅜in) for seam and hem allowances. Cut and join fabric widths to make two strips twice the length of **A** by the frill width, and two strips twice the length of **B** by the frill width; match any pattern across seams of joined widths.

MAKING THE BEDSPREAD

1 Joining the gusset panels Right sides together, pin and stitch the short edges of the gusset panels into a loop, alternating end and side panels so the seams line up with the corners of the central panel.

2 Attaching the piping Make two strips of covered piping, each the overall length of the gusset plus 2.5cm (1in) for overlaps. Matching the raw edges and with right sides together, tack one piping strip around the central panel and the other around the lower edge of the gusset. For ease and a neat finish, snip into the piping seam allowance at the corners.

3 Hemming the frill Turn under and press a 1cm (⅜in) double hem along the lower edge and side edges of each frill strip, mitring the corners for a neat finish. Machine stitch the hem in place.

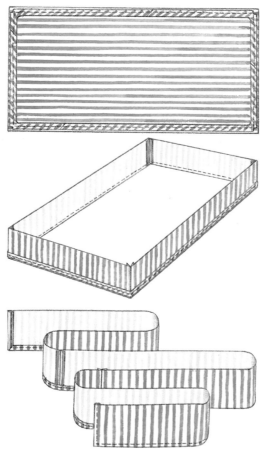

4 Sectioning the frill Divide the long gusset panels into three equal sections, and the short panels into two equal sections, marking the divisions with pins along the piped edge. Measure and mark the corresponding frill pieces into the same number of sections.

5 Stitching the gathering Stopping and starting the stitches at the section marks, work two parallel rows of gathering stitches 1.2cm (½in) and 2cm (¾in) in from the raw edges of the frills.

6 Attaching the frills With right sides together and matching the raw edges, pin the frill sections to the corresponding gusset panels at the section marks. Pull up the gathering stitches to fit, then pin and tack the frill and gusset together. Using a zip foot, stitch the frills in place close to the piping cord. Remove the gathering stitches.

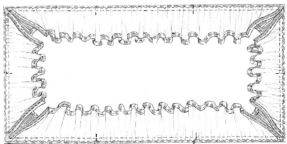

7 Attaching the gusset
With right sides together, matching the raw edges and the gusset seams to the corners, pin and tack the gusset around the central panel. Using a zip foot, stitch the gusset in place, close to the piping cord. Neaten the seam allowances with machine zigzag stitch.

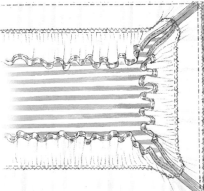

MAKING A FRILLED BEDSPREAD

These instructions show you how to make a traditional fitted bedspread with a full, gathered skirt stitched around three sides to cover the bedbase. You need the same materials to make this bedspread as for the gusseted version.

1 **Measuring up and cutting out** Measure the length (**A**) and width (**B**) of the bed with the bedclothes in place. Add 3.5cm (1⅜in) to the length and 3cm (1¼in) to the width for seam and hem allowances. Following step 1, *Cutting the Fabric*, cut and join fabric widths to make up a rectangle this size.

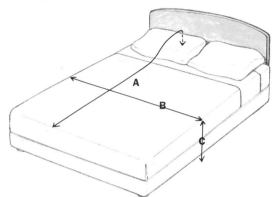

2 **Cutting the skirt** Measure the skirt depth (**C**) from the top of the bed to the floor plus 3.5cm (1⅜in) for hem and seam allowances. Measure the skirt length around the sides and foot of the bed, adding 24cm (9½in) so the skirt will wrap around at the bedhead. Multiply the length by two. Cut and join fabric widths to make up a strip this size.

3 **Hemming the panels** Press under a double 1cm (⅜in) hem along the head end of the central panel, and along the lower and side edges of the skirt, neatly mitring the corners. Machine stitch the hems in place.

4 **Attaching the piping** Make up a strip of covered piping to go round the sides and foot of the central panel plus 24cm (9½in). Matching the raw edges, tack the piping around the right side of the central panel, so that it extends for 12cm (4¾in) at either side of the head end. For a neat finish, snip into the piping seam allowance at the corners.

5 **Sectioning the skirt** Measure the length of the skirt and divide it into eight equal sections, marking each section with a pin at the raw edge. Measure and mark the piped edge of the central panel into the same number of sections as the skirt.

6 **Gathering the skirt** Following steps 5 and 6, *Making the Bedspread*, gather the skirt and stitch it around the piped edge of the central panel. Neaten the seam allowances using machine zigzag stitch.

◤ *A piped trim sewn around the central panel of the bedspread serves to define the seamline, emphasizing the neat, fitted shape.*

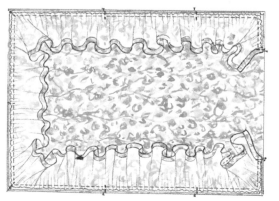

Perfect piping

Piping is a fabric-covered cord that adds a neat finish and strengthens the seam lines of cushions, tiebacks and other soft furnishings.

Covering a length of piping cord with fabric isn't difficult. You can buy plain and ready-covered piping by the metre or yard, but colours are limited. So it often makes sense to cover your own with exactly the fabric you want.

Piping cord comes in a range of sizes from the thinnest, 2mm/$\frac{1}{16}$in diameter (number 00) to the thickest, 6mm/$\frac{1}{4}$in diameter (6). (Numbers 3-5 are the sizes commonly used in soft furnishings.)

As a general guide, the smaller the item, the thinner the piping cord. For example, for a pincushion you would use a thin piping cord, a thicker cord would be suitable for piping floor length curtains.

Pre-shrunk piping cord must be used. It is especially important on large items of soft furnishings, such as loose covers, to avoid the item puckering at the seams when it is laundered.

When buying the cord, check to see if it has been pre-shrunk. If not, you will need to shrink it before using it.

To shrink piping cord, place it in a saucepan, cover with water and boil for five minutes. Remove and dry before use. As shrinkage can be as much as 10%, buy extra cord to accommodate it.

Covering fabric for piping cord must be cut on the fabric bias (the cross grain of the fabric) and be of a similar weight to the main fabric covering the article. Avoid loosely woven or light fabrics as the cord may show through.

To gauge the width of the covering strip, measure round the piping cord with a tape measure and allow an extra 3cm (1¼in) for seam allowances. To cover the middle range of piping cords, you'll need to cut a fabric strip about 5cm (2in) wide. Measure the length you need and allow an extra 10cm (4in) for joining.

Materials and tools for covering piping cord include:
- ❖ Piping cord
- ❖ Covering fabric
- ❖ Piping or zipper foot attachment
- ❖ Tape measure
- ❖ Sharp scissors
- ❖ Pins, needle, thread
- ❖ Strip of card (cardboard)
- ❖ Dressmaker's chalk

The choice of piping fabric determines the look of the piped edge: from the top, velvet gives a luxurious edging; lightweight cotton can be gathered to give a ruched effect; the same cotton fabric (ungathered) gives a crisp, defined piping; and a striped fabric appears to spiral.

How to make covered piping

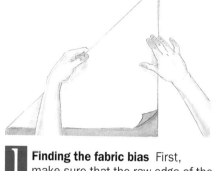

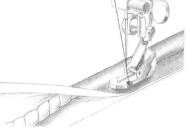

Plain cord for making covered piping is available in various thicknesses.

1 Finding the fabric bias First, make sure that the raw edge of the covering fabric is cut across the straight grain. Then fold the raw edge diagonally so the cut edge lies along the selvedge edge. Press along the diagonal fold to mark the fabric bias. Unfold the fabric. The strips are measured from both sides of the diagonal crease.

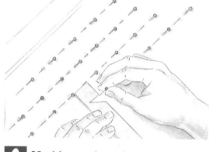

2 Marking and cutting the strips To ensure the strips are all the same width make a gauge. Cut a 4cm (1½ in) wide strip of card and cut out a notch at the required strip width. Lay the end against the diagonal fold and, using pins or chalk, mark the fabric along the straight edge of the notch.

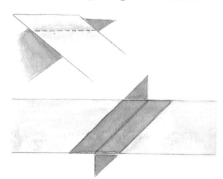

3 Joining the strips Bias strips must be joined together on the straight grain. Trim the ends along the straight grain of the fabric. Place the strips right sides together matching the cut ends. Pin and stitch taking 6mm (¼ in) seam allowance. Press the seam open and trim off points on either side of the strip.

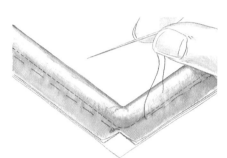

4 Covering the cord Fold the fabric strip evenly in half round the piping cord with wrong sides together. Pin and stitch down the length close to the cord. Use a piping or zipper foot attachment on the sewing machine to ensure stitching is close to the cord.

5 Positioning the piping Tack the piping on to the right side of one piece of fabric with the cord facing inwards and the raw edges of the piping strip matching the raw edges of the fabric. Start and stop tacking the piping 5cm (2in) from each end of the cord – this will make joining the ends together easier.

TIP

PIPING A CURVE

To help ease piping round a curved edge, clip into the seam allowance up to the stitching. For a good fit when turning a corner, tack the piping along the first side then clip into the allowance of the piping in line with the corner before taking the piping round to the next side.

6 Joining the cords To pipe a circular seam you join the two ends of the cord neatly where they come together. Unpick the cord stitching 5cm (2in) from the point where the cord ends will meet. Trim both cords so they butt together; secure with thread. Trim the covering fabric so one side overlaps the other by 2cm (¾ in). Turn under 1cm (⅜ in) and place over opposite raw edge. Pin and stitch over the join, matching up the stitching.

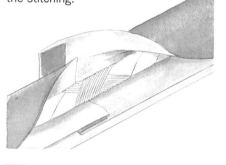

7 Neatening the piping cord end Unpick the cord stitching 2.5cm (1in) from the end of the seam and cut the piping cord to the exact length. Trim the fabric covering to 1cm (⅜ in) beyond the end of the cord. Tuck the fabric over the cut end of the cord to neaten and restitch the seam. At this stage, the covered piping is ready to stitch in place.

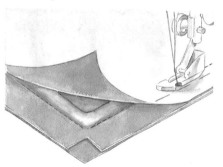

8 Completing the seam Once the cord is tacked in place and the ends neatened or joined, place the second fabric piece over the first with right sides together. Pin, tack and machine stitch in place close to the piping cord.

Introduction to quilting

Quilting is the traditional technique of stitching together layers of filling and fabric to create a decorative fabric with a textured surface. Simple running stitches, worked by hand or machine, anchor the sandwich of layers together.

quilting hoop

Types of batting

Fabrics

Top fabric Choose a smooth, light-to mediumweight fabric, with a firm, close weave, – furnishing cotton or cotton blends are ideal. Slippery fabrics such as silk and satin are difficult to handle, but worth considering as the sheen highlights the quilted design. If the item needs frequent laundering, select a washable preshrunk fabric. Both plain or printed fabrics are suitable. With a plain fabric, the quilting texture becomes the main feature. With a print, using the existing pattern as the basis of the quilted design is usually best.

Backing fabric The back layer of the quilt is usually made from a plain cotton of similar weight and care requirement as the top layer. For a bed quilt avoid a slippery backing.

Batting

Batting is the padding sandwiched between top and backing fabric. It is available in a variety of lofts (thicknesses). Low loft is easiest to handle and best for machine quilting; higher lofts are better suited to hand quilting.

Polyester wadding is washable, lightweight, easy to work with and uniformly thick and warm. It is available precut, or in widths up to 96cm (37¾in) and in a wide variety of lofts.

Cotton wadding is a traditional batting and most suitable for closely worked designs. It matts with washing so it requires dry cleaning.

Flannel, fleece, or lightweight blanket material provide light padding.

Iron-on backing (fleece) For projects that need little padding, use iron-on backing which comes printed with a range of patterns. Work from the wrong side of the quilting.

Marking designs

Quilting designs are marked on the top fabric before the layers are assembled.

Use **tailors' chalk, pencils** or **air-erasable pens** to mark the fabric. **Graph** and **tracing paper** are useful when you plan your own designs.

Use a **clear plastic ruler** for straight lines and a **pair of compasses** or a **French curve** for drawing curves.

Stencils and **templates** are available ready-made, or you can make your own from a sheet of firm card (cardboard).

Needles and threads

Use a good quality thread for durability and ease of stitching. Pick one which matches or contrasts with the fabric. For tacking, use a fine white cotton thread.

Hand-sewing needles Betweens (quilting needles) are short sharp needles you use with a thimble for tacking and handsewing. Sizes 8 or 9 are ideal for most quilting fabrics but you may need to go up or down a size with lighter or heavier fabrics.

Machine needles are chosen to suit the weight and thickness of the layers, from size 11/80 for thinner quilting, to 14/90 for thicker layers. Always start with a new needle.

Safety pins hold the layers together while tacking. They can also secure rolled up quilts for machine stitching. Use 2.5cm (1in) rustproof safety pins.

Quilting pins are extra long with a narrow shaft and usually are glass-headed.

Machine threads Use 100% cotton or cotton-coated polyester thread, number 40-50.

Hand-sewing threads Use 100% cotton or cotton-coated polyester thread, Perle cotton or glazed quilting thread. If you are not using glazed threads, prevent unglazed threads from tangling by running them through beeswax before using them.

Machine equipment

Work machine quilting with either a general purpose presser foot or a special quilting foot. These vary with different machine manufacturers, so always check your instruction manual.

A **clear, lightweight foot** is helpful for free machine quilting – the fabric moves freely and makes it easy to see where to stitch.

A **darning foot** is also useful for free quilting. For quilting in straight lines, attach a **quilting bar** to the foot.

Frames and hoops

For hand quilting the fabric is mounted on a frame or hoop to hold it taut.

Quilting hoops are available in sizes up to 56cm (22in) wide, sometimes with stands.

Quilting frames are large free-standing frames.

thimble

clear sewing machine foot

quilting bar

twin needle

pair of compasses

safety pins

hand-sewing needles

suitable fabric

clear ruler

quilting pins

felt tip pens

tailors' chalk

beeswax

Preparing to quilt

For both machine and hand quilting it is important to tack the layers securely together to keep the fabric layers aligned. For marking, pinning, tacking and stitching, work from the centre of the quilt out. Prevent puckering when tacking and stitching by working parallel lines in the same direction.

T I P

QUICK MARKING

A quick and easy way of marking out straight lines on resilient fabrics is to use masking tape. Position the tape on the fabric so that one edge marks the quilting line, and stitch along that edge. Peel off the tape and reuse for the next line.

Layering and tacking

For small projects pin and then tack the wadding, backing and main fabric together in one go. For large projects it is easier to tack the wadding to the backing, then tack them to the top fabric.

Tacking the layers Sandwich the batting between the top and backing fabric, right sides out, smoothing the

Cutting out After allowing for seams, cut out batting and fabric pieces, larger than the final item to allow for shrinkage during quilting. On average expect shrinkage, to both length and width, of about 10cm (4in). Cut batting and backing 5-10cm (2-4in) larger than the top fabric on all sides.

Joining the batting

To join widths of batting, overlap the edges and pin. Using scissors, cut through the middle of both layers. Remove the trimmed sections and butt the edges together. Join with herringbone stitch.

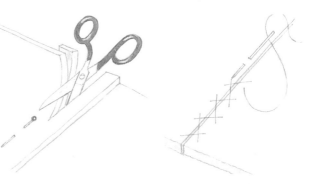

layers with a metre rule. Pin together. Tack together, working from the centre out, in regularly spaced lines about 10cm (4in) apart. Avoid puckering by working parallel tacking rows in the same direction. Align tacking stitches in a different way from quilting stitches, for example a horizontal and vertical grid for a diagonal quilted pattern.

Marking up Stretch the fabric out on a smooth, hard surface. Hold it flat and taut with masking tape at the edges or, alternatively, you can use bull-dog clips. Using a template or specialized quilting ruler as a guide, mark the fabric in tailors' chalk or an air-erasable pen with distinct but fine lines.

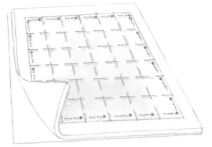

- -

Machine quilting

For large projects, quilting is quicker and easier using a machine. The stitches are more durable and the depth and texture of the quilting is accentuated. Use this method for both simple and more intricate designs.

❖ Loosen the stitch tension and use a long stitch: 4-5 stitches per cm (10-12 per in).

❖ Reduce pressure on the presser foot.

❖ For large quilted items, set the machine on a table so the fabric and the stitches will not pull when stitched. Roll or fold the quilt either side of the working area and secure with safety pins, so it doesn't hang over the edge of the sewing surface. Fold the remainder into concertina pleats and rest it on your lap.

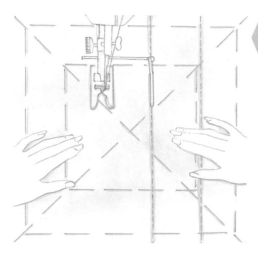

Guided machine quilting

This method works well for simple geometric designs. The fabric is guided through the machine with a presser foot. For regularly spaced parallel lines, reduce the amount of marking up by fitting a quilting bar.

Mark the first line at the centre of the quilt and tack layers together. Stitch along the marked line. Set the quilting bar guide to the chosen width, move quilt to align the bar with the stitched line and stitch parallel to it. Reposition to stitch the other lines of quilting.

Free machine quilting

This is best for free-flowing, curving designs.

To achieve this look, guide the fabric through the machine by hand, so you can stitch in any direction without having to reposition the quilt. Use a darning foot or stitch without a foot, referring to the manufacturer's instructions for your specific machine.

PATTERN QUILTING

Quilting is a wonderful way to highlight the motifs of a patterned fabric, while adding texture, body and — most importantly — warmth to a bedspread.

Q uilting is a traditional technique that has been used for many years to add warmth and a charming textured quality to fabrics. It involves stitching together three layers of fabric: a top layer, (often printed fabric), a middle insulating layer and a backing. You can use a sewing machine or work by hand.

The technique given here shows how to make a bedspread by machine quilting round an existing pattern in a printed fabric. Using a printed fabric, you don't need to mark up a pattern on the fabric, so it is an ideal first quilting project. However, before starting the bedspread

Read more about quilting on pages 13-14.

it is best to try the technique on something smaller, such as a cushion cover, which then makes an ideal accessory.

The technique is straightforward, and following certain guidelines makes the job even easier. Machine quilting is unsuitable for intricate, curved designs, and on a large item it is difficult to turn the fabric to stitch around tiny shapes. Select a print which has smooth, uncomplicated outlines. A striped pattern is particularly simple to stitch. It is not essential to quilt round all the print's motifs — effective results are achieved by highlighting just a few sections.

The circus wagons and broad coloured stripes of this bedspread are highlighted with quilting. This example demonstrates that it is not necessary to quilt every motif for a successful result.

MAKING A QUILTED BEDSPREAD

In this method you sew a lining to the underside of the bedspread, hiding the backing layer of the quilt and neatening the edges in the process. Alternative methods of finishing the edges with piping or binding are given on the next page.

Choose a firm, closely woven furnishing cotton for the top fabric, and team it with a coordinating lining fabric. Make sure both fabrics are easy to clean and preshrunk. Use an inexpensive preshrunk sheeting or plain cotton for the backing fabric.

When quilting an extra large item, such as a double bedspread, it is easier to work it in sections. Place the machine on a large table or worktop to give the fabric enough space. Don't let the fabric hang over the side of the work surface as the weight can prevent you from feeding the fabric under the machine foot.

YOU WILL NEED

❖ PATTERNED
  FURNISHING FABRIC

❖ WADDING – light to
  mediumweight
  50-100g (2-4oz)

❖ BACKING FABRIC

❖ LINING FABRIC

❖ METRE RULE/YARDSTICK

❖ MATCHING SEWING
  THREAD

❖ TAPE MEASURE

FABRIC AMOUNTS

Before you measure up the bed, decide what size of quilted bedspread you'd like – whether it is to reach the floor or to leave some of the valance (bed skirt) showing. As a guide, for a *standard double* bed 136cm (4ft 6in) wide, two lengths of 120cm (45in) wide furnishing fabric should be sufficient to give a bedspread with a drop either side of about 45cm (18in). The quilt illustrated below is a standard double bed quilt. A *single* bed also needs two lengths of fabric, while a *queen- or kingsize* bed requires at least three widths in total.

When joining fabric, position a full width of fabric so that it runs the centre of the bedspread and add the panels to each side.

 Measuring up Measure the bed with bedclothes in place. Measure width (**A**) from the chosen depth on one side, to the same depth on the other side. Measure length (**B**), from behind the pillow to the chosen depth at the bed foot. To tuck the bedspread in under a pillow, add an extra 30cm (12in) to the length. Add an extra 10cm (4in) to **A** and **B** for hems and to compensate for the shrinkage of the quilting.

2 **Cutting out** For the main piece cut one full width of fabric to length **B**.
Single and double beds Cut a second width to length **B** plus extra to allow for pattern matching, then cut it in half lengthways.
Queen- and kingsize beds Cut three lengths **B**. Do not cut the panels in half.

3 **Trimming to size** Lay the panels flat, overlapping 1.5cm (⅝in) seams. If their combined width is more than **A**, trim an even amount from the width of each narrower panel (single/double beds) or from the outer lengths (queen/kingsize beds). Unpin panels. Cut wadding and backing to size of trimmed panels.

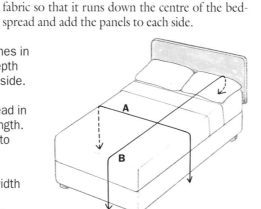

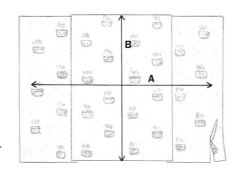

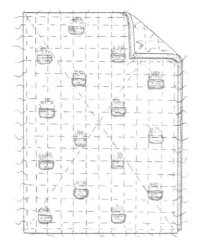

4 **Stacking the quilt layers** Keep the layers for each bedspread panel separate as you quilt each panel individually. Lay the backing fabric on a large, flat work surface. Place the wadding and then the top fabric, right side up, on to the backing, keeping the layers as smooth as possible. Smooth out the fabric with a metre stick.

5 **Tacking the layers** Working from the centre out, pin, then tack the layers together. Tack from the centre diagonally to each corner and then in a horizontal and vertical grid with tacking lines spaced 10cm (4in) apart. Pin and tack around the outer edges of the quilt. Remove the pins.

BUDGET BEDSPREAD
If two lengths of fabric are not quite enough to make up the bedspread, rather than buy a third length of fabric add a deep border in a contrasting fabric to the outer edge.

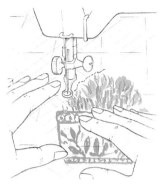
A beautiful quilted bedspread makes a perfect centrepiece for your bedroom. Large motifs with smooth outlines are the simplest to quilt and have a vivid impact.

7 Starting to quilt
Work from the centre out, quilting around each motif at an even speed. Leave outer 5cm (2in) of each quilted panel unstitched. At corners, leave the needle in the fabric and pivot fabric to sew in different direction. Always sew parallel lines in the same direction.

8 Continuing the quilting Adjust the position of the bedspread, unrolling and re-rolling to reveal unquilted areas as you go. Take in any loose threads to the wrong side. When the quilting is complete, remove the tacking stitches. Repeat steps 6-8 for each panel.

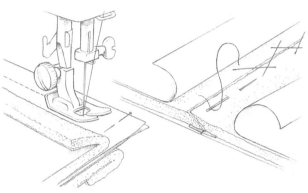

9 Joining the panels Refit the presser foot. Pin the top layers of the quilted sections together with right sides facing and stitch only the top fabric pieces together taking 1.5cm (⅝in) seams. Trim then press the seams on top fabric open. Trim excess wadding, mitring it so the edges butt together along the seamline, and herringbone stitch together. Overlap backing fabric and slipstitch together. Handstitch quilting lines that cross seamlines.

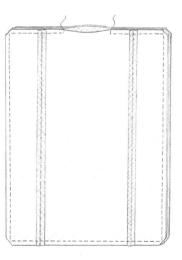

10 Attaching lining
Cut the lining to the same size as the top fabric, joining widths with 1.5cm (⅝in) seams. Lay the bedspread flat and, with right sides together, centre the lining over it. Pin and stitch a 1.5cm (⅝in) seam round the outer edge leaving a 45cm (18in) opening in the centre of one edge.

11 Completing the bedspread Trim away the excess wadding from seams and turn bedspread to the right side. Turn in the raw edges of the opening and slipstitch closed. To keep the lining in place, tack then topstitch round the bedspread 2cm (¾in) from the edge.

6 Preparing to quilt
Remove the presser foot or fit a darning foot. Check the tension on a scrap of fabric and wadding. Working on one panel at a time, roll both sides towards the centre, keeping the central area exposed. Secure the rolls with safety pins. Slide one roll of fabric under the arm of the sewing machine.

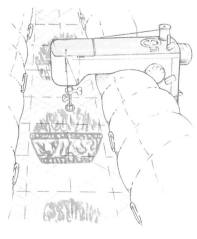

TRIMMING A QUILTED BEDSPREAD

A piped or bound edge gives a plump bedspread a well-defined edge and helps the quilt keep its shape. For the piping, choose a fabric that highlights one of the colours of the motifs or use a self trim.

▶ For more information on piping see pages 11-12.

PIPED EDGE

1 Making the piping Make up the bedspread following steps 1-9, pages 16-17. Measure all round outer edge of quilt, adding 10-15cm (4-6in) for joining, and make up a length of fabric-covered cord to this length.

▶ *A piped trim gives this bedspread a neat, well-defined finish.*

2 Stitching the piping Lay the bedspread right side up. Pin and tack piping around the edge, with the cord facing inwards and raw edges even. Stitch the piping in place, butt joining the ends. Clip piping at corner.

3 Attaching the lining Make up the lining to the same size as the bedspread. Pin, tack and sew lining in place, without topstitching, following steps 10 and 11, page 17.

BOUND EDGE

1 Cutting the binding Make up the bedspread following steps 1-9 of *Making a Quilted Bedspread* on the previous page. Cut the lining to the same size and, wrong sides together, sew a 1.5cm (⅝in) seam all round the edge. Measure all four sides of the bedspread, adding 3cm (1¼in) to the short edges for overlaps. Cut four binding strips, on the straight grain, to these lengths by twice the desired binding width, plus 3cm (1¼in) for seams.

2 Binding the long edges Press under 1.5cm (⅝in) on both long edges of the binding. Fold the binding in half lengthways and press. Open out the long binding strips. With right sides together and raw edges even, pin the binding to the long edges of the bedspread. Stitch a 1.5cm (⅝in) seam through all thicknesses. Fold the binding to the back of the bedspread and slipstitch along the pressed edge.

3 Binding the short edges Sew the remaining binding to the short edges in the same way. Stop stitching at either end, where they meet the long binding strips. Fold the binding to the back, forming neat mitres at the corners, and slipstitch in place.

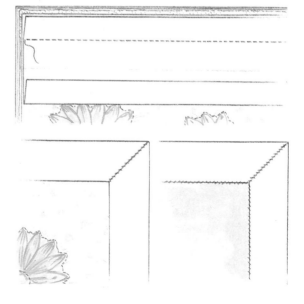

TIE-QUILTED BED THROW

This tie-quilted throw is just the right weight to use as a warm-weather bedcover. Backed with a coordinating fabric, it is completely reversible and very versatile as a result,.

The basic throw is quick to make as it needs very little machine stitching. Mediumweight wadding is sandwiched between two layers of fabric and, apart from joining fabric widths, the only machine stitching required is to attach the border, made from a padded, plain fabric strip. The quilted effect is created by hand stitching the fabric layers together at intervals. The quilted points are defined by button tufts, made from knotted embroidery cotton and hand stitched in place.

This style of throw dresses a bed in a smart, unfussy way and, unlike other more bulky covers, it is easy to incorporate into your scheme when not in use. You can simply fold the throw neatly at the end of the bed to use as a comforter, or drape it over a sofa or chair.

While you can make the throw to any size, this example is designed to be used with a valance (bed skirt), so it does not need to hang right down to the floor to hide the bed base or legs. For the best effect, make the throw large enough to just overhang the valance all round. You can team the throw with a quilted valance, as shown, for a neat, contemporary look, or use it with a gathered one for a country-style room. For instructions on making the quilted valance see pages 37-38.

A reversible tie-quilted throw provides lightweight comfort, and has the tailored good looks to suit most bedroom styles.

Read more on quilting on pages 13-14.

19

MAKING THE THROW

Closely woven, washable cotton and cotton-mix fabrics are the best choice for the throw. Use equal weight fabrics throughout – ideally from a coordinating range – so that they handle in the same way. Use polyester wadding for the padding as this is washable and easy to sew.

If you need to join widths, allow for a panel to run centrally down the bed, as this looks more attractive than a central seam. Ideally, choose checks, stripes or other patterned fabrics, so that seams won't be as noticeable. For the basic throw you need equal amounts of the top and reverse side fabrics, plus wadding.

The border is made from 10cm (4in) wide toning plain fabric and wadding strips, joined together to fit round the throw. When estimating amounts for the border, plan to cut the strips from across the fabric and wadding width.

1 Cutting out the throw Measure the mattress length (**A**) and add on twice depth (**B**). Measure the width (**C**) and add on twice depth (**B**). Add on an extra 30cm (12in) to both measurements to allow for the bulk created by bedding. This is the size of the throw. Cut out the top and backing fabrics and wadding to these measurements, joining widths as necessary.

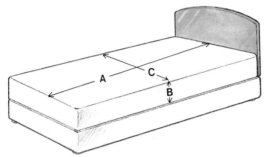

2 Cutting the border Measure round the edge of the throw. Cut and join 10cm (4in) wide strips of plain fabric to this length plus 80cm (31½in) for mitred corners. Press seams open. Join wadding strips to give a strip the same size.

3 Securing the layers Lay out the main fabric with the right side down and place the wadding on top. With the wrong side down, lay the backing fabric on the wadding. Pin then tack the layers together, working from the centre outwards.

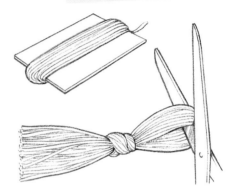

4 Marking the tie points On one side measure and mark the centre with tailors' chalk. Working out from the centre, measure and mark the tie points in a grid at roughly 40cm (15¾in) intervals. For a single bed throw, mark three tie points across and five down. Increase the number of tie points for larger sizes. To secure the fabric layers, use a double thread to hand stitch through all the layers at the marked points.

☑ *Team the tie-quilted throw with a quilted valance (bed skirt) to give a softly tailored look.*

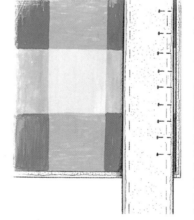

5 Making tufts Cut a 14cm (5½in) long piece of card and wind embroidery cotton around it lengthways 20 times. Slip the cotton off the card, keeping the loops together. Tie a knot halfway across the loops, then cut through the ends and trim them level. Stitch through the knot to attach a tuft to each quilted point on one side of the throw. Repeat on the reverse side.

6 Adding the border Tack the wadding to the wrong side of the border. Right sides facing, pin and tack the padded border round the throw, 1cm (⅜in) in from the raw edges. Fold the corners into neat mitres and tack. Machine stitch round, then trim away excess wadding from the seam allowance.

7 Completing the border Turn the throw over. Press in 1cm (⅜in) along the raw border edge and trim away excess wadding from the seam allowance. Position the folded edges in line with the previous stitching, folding the corners into neat mitres and pin. Slipstitch the border and corners in place.

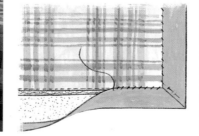

HAND-APPLIQUED BEDLINEN

Add folksy charm to plain white bedlinen with these sweet bird motifs.
They're simply appliquéd in place, then enhanced with decorative stitching in
soft embroidery cottons.

E ach bird is made up of three fabric pieces – two wings and a body – appliquéd in place on the sheet or pillowcase, then finished with decorative embroidery around the edges in soft cotton thread. The beak, legs, feet and eye are also embroidered, and a border of running stitches worked along the edges of the bedlinen completes the effect.

You don't need much in the way of materials to copy this charming design – just three or four coordinating cotton fabrics and a few skeins of embroidery

cotton. Choose small-scale, unfussy fabric designs, such as gingham and country-style mini-prints. Pick out colours from the fabrics for the embroidery thread, or choose a different complementary shade, like the pink used around the birds' bodies here. Keep to bright orange, yellow or red for the beak, legs and feet to add a splash of colour.

If you have any fabric and threads left-over after completing the bedlinen, you can use them to work the design on other plain items in the bedroom – a dressing gown, laundry bag or cushion cover, for example.

Use simple, country-style fabrics for the appliquéd birds to enhance their homespun appeal. Here, small-scale gingham is mixed with two cotton mini-prints, all in fresh blue and white.

Appliqued Sheet

You can work just one or a whole row of appliquéd birds along the top edge of a flat sheet. Position them all facing the same way, or flip the template so that some are facing each other. Remember to place the birds with their feet towards the top edge of the sheet so they'll be the right way up when you fold the sheet back.

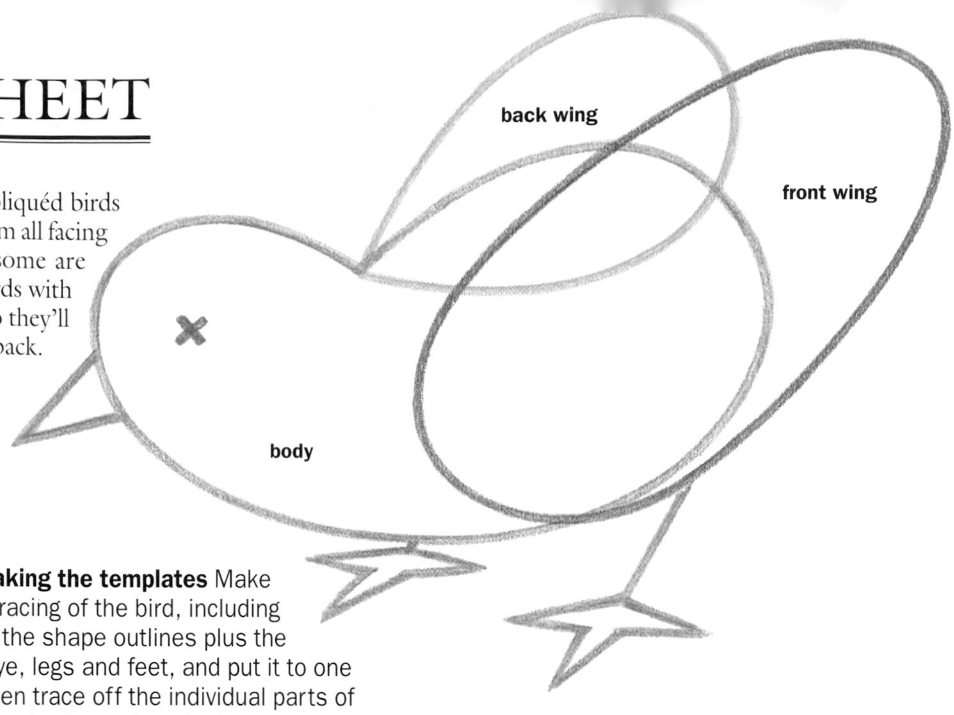

You Will Need

- Flat Sheet
- Scraps of Cotton Printed Fabrics
- Tracing Paper
- Pencil
- Thin Card (Cardboard)
- Dressmakers' Carbon Paper
- Water-soluble Marker Pen
- Matching Sewing Threads
- Sewing Needle and Pins
- Crewel Embroidery Needle, size 5
- DMC Soft Cotton in rust, pink, dark blue and white, or other colours of your choice
- Small Embroidery Hoop

Appliqué flanged pillowcases to match the sheet for a fully coordinated look, and finish them with a running-stitch border worked just inside the outer edges.

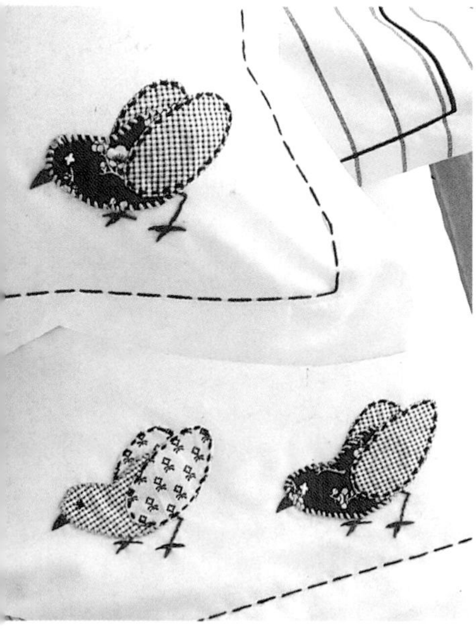

1 Making the templates Make a tracing of the bird, including all the shape outlines plus the beak, eye, legs and feet, and put it to one side. Then trace off the individual parts of the bird – the front wing, the back wing and the body – and transfer them on to the thin card. Cut them out to make templates.

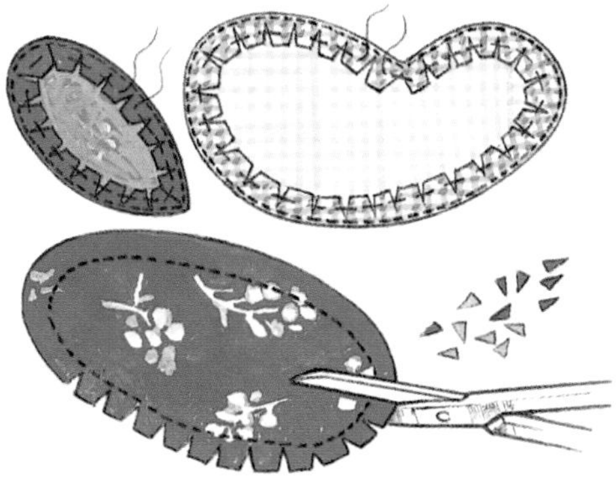

2 Cutting out the shapes For each bird, use the marking pen to draw around the templates to mark a front and back wing and one body on to the right side of the fabrics; remember to flip the templates for birds facing the opposite way. Mark a 6mm (¼in) turning allowance all round each shape, then cut out the shapes roughly just beyond this allowance.

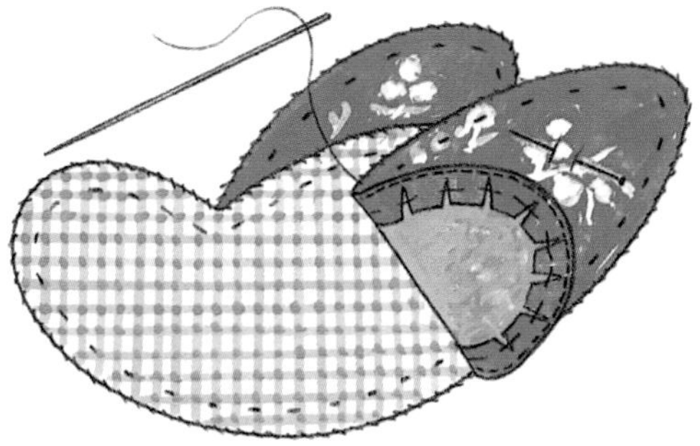

3 Hemming the shapes Stitch around each shape just beyond the *inner* outline with small running or machine stitches to reinforce it. Trim each shape along the *outer* marked line and clip into the allowance up to the stitched line at inner and outer curves. Finger press then tack the turnings to the wrong side so the stitched line is just out of view. Group together the shapes for each bird.

4 Stitching the birds Lay the tracing of the bird outline on the sheet in the desired position for the first bird, and secure with pins. Slip a back wing under the tracing, lining up the outlines, and pin it in place. Remove the tracing and slipstitch around the edges of the back wing. Repeat to position and stitch the body then the front wing in place. Repeat for each bird. Remove the tacking stitches and pins. Steam press the appliqué lightly under a clean cloth.

5 Transferring the markings Position and pin the tracing of the bird outline over one bird. Slip a piece of dressmakers' carbon paper underneath and transfer the markings for the beak, eye, legs and feet. Repeat for each bird.

6 Embroidering the birds Using the embroidery hoop, soft cotton and crewel needle, work running stitches in blue round the wings, and oversewn stitches in pink round the bodies. Using orange cotton, embroider the beaks in satin stitch, the legs in stem stitch and the feet in straight stitches. Work a blue cross stitch for each eye. Work long running stitches along the machined hem at the top edge of the sheet. Press as before.

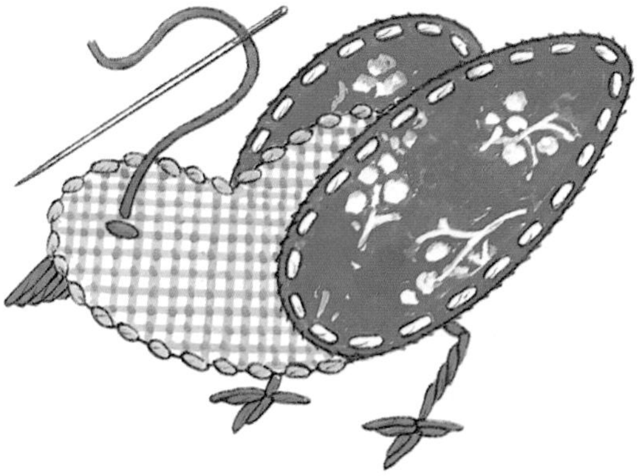

Embroidery stitches

Embroidery stitches are the building bricks of embroidery design.

This introduction to embroidery stitches shows how to work a range of the most useful stitches. If you master these basic stitches you will soon be able to work quite complex designs.

Before embarking on a complete embroidered design, try out any stitches you are unfamiliar with on a scrap of embroidery fabric. For worked examples of the stitches below see over the page.

SECURING THREADS

Be sure that the thread is secured with a small backstitch at the beginning and end of your stitching.

To work backstitch, bring the threaded needle from the back to the front of the fabric, leaving a short length of thread loose at the back. Hold the loose end securely and make a small stitch backwards, bringing the needle to the front of the fabric just behind the emerging thread. Take the needle to the back of the fabric again by stitching backwards into the same hole and continue in your chosen embroidery stitch. If possible, work the first embroidery stitch so that it conceals the backstitch.

When you require new thread, change colour or have completed the design, secure with backstitch. Finish with the thread at the back of the fabric.

Basic chain stitch

One of the most popular embroidery stitches, chain stitch (**A**) is used for outlining or filling in designs. As a filling stitch work in close rows in the same direction, or in a spiral from the centre out.

1 **Looping the thread** Bring the needle to the front of the fabric and then insert it back near the same hole. With the thread looped under the point of the needle, bring the needle out a short distance away along the stitching line. Pull stitch through so that the loop lies completely flat.

2 **Working a chain** Repeat along the stitching line, inserting needle back through the hole it has just emerged from for each stitch. Secure the final loop with a small stitch over it into the back of the fabric.

Lazy daisy (detached chain stitch)

Lazy daisy (**B**) is used as an individual detail, or worked in a circular group to make a flower, with each stitch forming a petal.

Working separate chain stitches Start each stitch at the centre of the flower design and securing each loop with a small stitch. Bring the needle out at the centre of the pattern to start the next stitch.

Basic backstitch

Backstitch (**C**) is used for outlining or as a baseline for other decorative stitches.

1 **Making the first stitch** Working from right to left, bring the needle to the front of the fabric and take a small stitch backwards. Bring the needle to the front of the fabric ahead of the first stitch, keeping the distance between backward and forward stitches even.

2 **Stitching a line** Create a row of stitches following the pattern line by taking another stitch backwards, inserting the needle through the same hole as the previous stitch.

Stem stitch

Stem stitch (**D**) is used for outlining or as a decorative pattern for working stems. Worked in close rows it is also used as a filling in stitch.

1 **Forming the stitch** Working from left to right along the line of the design, bring the needle to the front of the fabric. Take a long stitch forwards and, holding the thread to one side of the emerging needle, make a shorter one backwards to the middle of the previous stitch.

Split stitch

Split stitch (**E**) is worked with stranded cotton and used for outlining, or as solid rows for filling in. It is similar to stem stitch, except when the needle emerges, it splits the thread.

Working from left to right, bring needle to the front of the fabric. Take a long stitch forwards and a shorter one backwards, so that the emerging needle splits the thread of the previous stitch. Repeat to stitch a row.

2 **Stitching a row** Repeat the stitch by taking another stitch backwards. Bring the needle out through the same hole as the previous stitch. Keep the stitches even and the thread to the same side of the needle each time.

Satin stitch

Satin stitch (**F**) is used to create a smooth surface when filling in designs. Work straight parallel lines across the shape of the design so that none of the fabric shows.

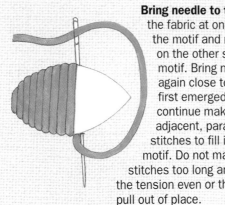

Bring needle to the front of the fabric at one edge of the motif and re-insert it on the other side of the motif. Bring needle up again close to where it first emerged and continue making adjacent, parallel stitches to fill in the motif. Do not make stitches too long and keep the tension even or they may pull out of place.

Slanted satin stitch

Slanted satin stitch (**G**) is worked in the same way as basic satin stitch, with the stitches set at an angle to the motif shape.

Start the stitches at the centre of the motif to establish the angle of the slant. Work one half of the design from the centre of the motif out, and then go back to the centre and work the other half of the motif in the opposite direction to fill the motif completely.

Filling stitches/detached stitches

These stitches are all worked separately. They are used to fill in a design area, creating a bobbly texture, or to form individual decorative features.

Seeding stitch

Seeding stitch (**H**) is the simplest filler stitch. It can be used singly or in clusters and is often used for shading.

Bring the needle to the front of the fabric and take a tiny stitch. Repeat individual stitches across the fabric. Change direction of stitches to get a textured effect. For closer coverage, repeat adding a second tiny stitch parallel to each of the first ones.

French knots

Small raised stitches, French knots (**I**) add surface interest. When worked close together they give a knobbly texture.

1 **Forming the knot** Bring the needle to the front of the fabric. Holding the thread taut, wrap it twice anti-clockwise round the needle,

2 **Fixing the knot** Keeping the thread taut, insert the needle back into the fabric, next to the point where it first came through. Pull needle through and secure with backstitch.

Bullion knots

Bullion knots (**J**) can be used as filling or outlining stitches. Worked in a spiral they form the petals of a rose design.

1 **Winding the thread** Bring needle to the front of the fabric and make a small backstitch. Before drawing the needle fully out of the fabric at the front, wrap the thread five to seven times around it. Pull needle gently through fabric and thread coil, holding the coil flat against the fabric.

2 **Securing the knot** Pull working thread tight and use point of needle to pack coil threads evenly. Insert needle in the fabric at the end of the coil and work backstitch to secure.

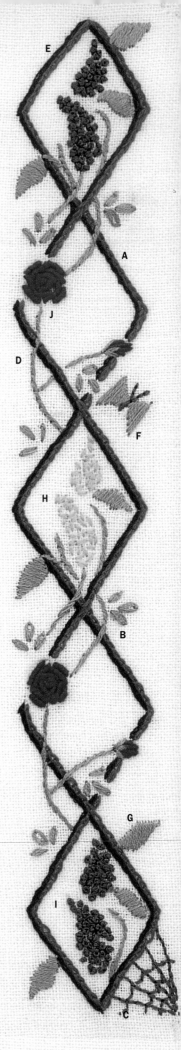

Duvet Covers

By making your own duvet cover and pillowcases, you can mix and match the fabrics so that they complement the overall colour scheme of your bedroom perfectly.

A duvet cover is easy to make because it is basically a large, rectangular bag with a fastening at one end. Sewing pillowcases to match or complement your new duvet cover completes the new look for your bedlinen.

When choosing the fabric, remember that the bed is probably the largest piece of furniture in the room, so that the duvet cover automatically becomes a focal point. Light colours give a fresh, pretty look while rich, dark colours create a warmer, more sophisticated mood.

You can use the same fabric for both sides of the cover, or choose a different one

Read more about French seams on page 32 and frills on pages 29-30.

for each side. A reversible cover is an interesting option, as you can mix plain and printed fabrics or contrasting colours and change the look of your bed in an instant by turning the duvet over. Decorative trimmings such as ribbons and lace add an extra touch of luxury.

Bedlinen has to be practical as well as pretty. Pure cotton and polyester-cotton mixes are popular choices for duvet covers because they are machine-washable and reasonably inexpensive. Look out for polyester-cotton sheeting fabric which comes in a wide range of plain colours and coordinating prints.

The main advantage of making your own duvet cover is that you can choose fabrics that tie in exactly with existing furnishings. The vibrant checks and florals used here create an exciting scheme.

25

MAKING A BASIC DUVET COVER

Cut the cover pieces to the same size as the duvet, so that it looks plump and inviting. The standard duvet cover sizes are: single 135 x 200cm (54 x 78in), double 200 x 200cm (78 x 78in) and kingsize 230 x 220cm (90 x 86in). Check that your duvet conforms to one of these standard measurements before you start to cut

out any of the fabric.

Sheeting is 230cm (90in) wide, which means that it is wide enough to cover one side of a kingsize duvet. With narrower fabrics, you need to join strips to obtain the correct width. Avoid an unsightly centre seam by joining a narrow fabric strip to either side of a full fabric width.

1 Cutting out and hemming Cut a rectangle for front, and one for back – each measuring the width of duvet plus 4cm (1½in) for seams, by the length plus 7cm (2¾in) for seams and hem. Turn under a double 2.5cm (1in) hem along lower edge of each rectangle. Pin then machine stitch.

2 Preparing the fastener Cut a length of press fastener tape for the opening – 100cm (39½in) for a single duvet, 150cm (59in) for a double and 160cm (63in) for a kingsize. Undo the fastening and pin one part centrally to the right side of each cover piece along the hem.

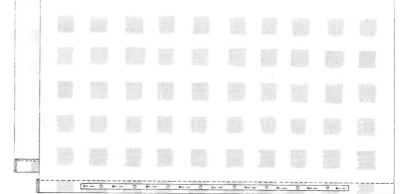

3 Stitching the fastening Place cover pieces together to check the press fasteners correspond and adjust position of press fastener tape if necessary. Carefully pull the fastener tape apart. Turn under 1cm (⅜in) at the raw ends of the press fastener tape and, using a zipper foot, machine stitch both long edges, close to the edge of the tape.

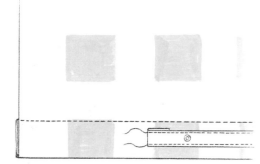

4 Finishing the opening Press the two sides of the fastening tape together. At either end of the fastening tape, pin and tack cover pieces together just above the hem, from the duvet raw edge to 1.5cm (⅝in) past the end of tape. Then tack at right angles across the hem and tape. Machine stitch along tacking lines, stitching twice across the hem and tape.

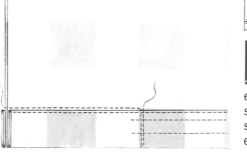

5 Completing the cover Use French seams. With wrong sides together stitch three remaining edges taking a 1cm (⅜in) seam. Trim seams to 5mm (¼in). Turn to wrong side and stitch a 1cm (⅜in) seam to enclose raw edges. Turn to right side.

ADDING A FRILL

Adding a gathered frill to the basic duvet cover is very straightforward. For a reversible duvet cover it is better to use a strip of lace, as in this method, or make a double frill so that the cover looks neat from both sides.

You can attach a frill to the sides of the cover, to the sides and lower edge, or all the way around the cover as shown here.

1 Cutting out Cut out and hem the front and back cover pieces as in step 1 for the *Basic Duvet Cover*. Measure round the four sides of the duvet and cut frill strips, one and a half times this measurement. Join them into a loop.

2 Attaching frill Run rows of gathering stitches, 3mm (⅛in) from either side of frill seam line. Divide both the edges of cover front and the frill into the same number of equal-sized sections and mark with pins. Matching pins and raw edges, pin frill to right side of cover front, side and top edges. On opening edge, pin frill 1.5cm (⅝in) in from hemmed edge. Gather frill to fit and tack.

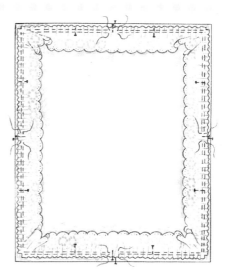

3 **Completing cover** Prepare and attach the fastening tape as in steps 3 and 4, *Basic Duvet Cover*. The front tape piece covers the raw edge of the frill. Finish the opening and join the cover as given in steps 4 and 5, catching the frill in between the two layers. Remove gathering stitches.

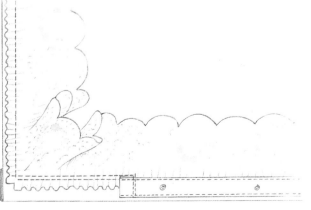

◣ *This crisp white duvet cover and matching pillowcases are made in an inexpensive sheeting cotton and trimmed with a broderie anglaise frill for a delicate feminine touch.*

MAKING A BASIC PILLOWCASE

A matching or coordinating pillowcase completes the bedding ensemble. Plain pillowcases, made from one rectangle, are simple to sew and a frill is an easy and attractive addition.

YOU WILL NEED

❖ FABRIC
❖ SCISSORS
❖ MATCHING THREAD
❖ LACE FRILL (optional)

1 Cutting out and hemming Cut out a rectangle of fabric, the width of the pillow plus 4cm (1½in), by twice the length of pillow plus 24cm (9½in).

2 Hemming and folding Machine a double 1cm (⅜in) hem on one short end. On the remaining short end, turn under a 5mm (¼in), then 3.5cm (1⅜in) hem and machine in place. Bringing wrong sides together, fold and press under the 1cm (⅜in) hem end by 15cm (6in). Fold the remaining hemmed edge to meet the pressed edge.

3 Stitching edges Pin and stitch raw edges taking a 1cm (⅜in) seam. Trim seams to 5mm (¼in). Turn to wrong side and stitch a 1cm (⅜in) seam to enclose raw edges. Turn case to right side.

- -

A FRILLED PILLOWCASE

1 Cutting out For the front, cut a rectangle of fabric the pillow width plus 3cm (1¼in) by the length plus 3cm (1¼in). For the back, cut a rectangle 1.5cm (⅝in) longer. Cut a separate flap, 20cm (8in) deep by the width of pillow plus 3cm (1¼in).

2 Making the frill Measure the four sides of pillow and cut frill strips one and a half times this measurement. Join them together. Follow instructions for making up and attaching a double frill, steps 2-5, page 92.

☑ *Frilled pillowcases complete the colourful bedlinen collection, made to your own shape and style, or available ready-made.*

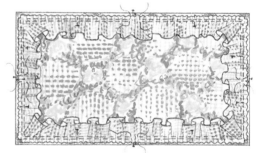

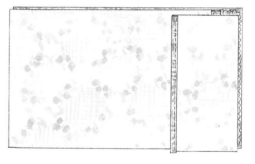

3 Stitching the case Stitch a double 1.5cm (⅝in) hem on one short end of the back piece. Stitch a double 1cm (⅜in) hem on one long edge of flap. With right sides together and raw edges even, place back and front together. Position flap, right side down, over the back hemmed edge, matching front and flap raw edges. Stitch outer edges. Zigzag stitch or bind seams to neaten.

All about frills

Single, folded, layered, lacy, shaped, piped – there's a frill to add extra appeal to

[handwritten: PILLOW CASE   Stitch on FRILL P. 29]

A frill is a strip of fabric gathered along one edge, which is used to soften and decorate the hard edge of a variety of soft furnishings, from cushions and curtains to tablecloths and bedlinen.

Frill choice A single frill is the easiest option, but a double frill made from folded fabric is the best choice where both sides of the frill are seen. For a fancier effect, consider a layered frill made up of two or more gathered strips – one of the layers can be lace for a very pretty feminine finish.

Choosing the fabric The simplest choice is to make a frill in the same fabric as the item to be trimmed – if it is patterned, for example with a stripe, experiment by running the frill pattern in a different direction to the main fabric.

To be more adventurous, choose a matching, contrasting or toning fabric of a similar or lighter weight – glazed chintz is usually ideal. A layered frill can have two contrasting fabrics, or one layer of fabric and another of lace. When choosing your frill fabric, also think about whether you want to finish the frill with a simple hem, or add a contrasting binding or piping as well.

If you are using different fabrics, check that they are compatible as far as cleaning is concerned.

Fabric amounts The length of the strip depends on the weight of the fabric, and how full you want the gathers to be.

Generally, mediumweight material requires a strip 2½ times the final length required; light fabrics a strip 3 times the final length, and heavy fabrics a strip twice the length required.

If you need to join strips together to get the required length, add a seam allowance of 3cm (1¼in) for each join and, for a neat finish, join the lengths with French or flat fell seams.

To your chosen depth, add a combined hem and seam allowance of 3cm (1¼in).

Sewing a single frill

1 Cutting out Cut out the strips on the straight grain and join them as necessary.

2 Hemming Turn under a double 6mm (¼in) hem on lower and side edges of the frill. For a frill to trim a circular or a square shape, such as a cushion, join the strips into a ring before hemming them.

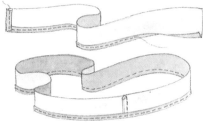

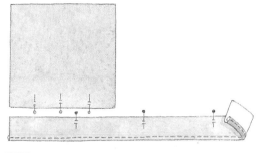

3 Marking To ensure that the gathers are even, divide the frill into manageable sections no greater than 1m (1⅛ yd), then divide the item to be trimmed into the same number of sections, marking sections with pins or a coloured tacking stitch. For a frill to go around a corner, the frill section should be slightly longer than the matching edge section, to allow for extra gathers around the corner.

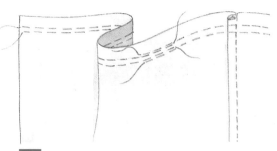

4 Stitching the gathering Set the machine to the largest straight stitch, or work running stitch by hand, and sew two parallel rows of stitching 6mm (¼in) apart. To make it easier to draw up the threads without them breaking, stitch in manageable sections no longer than 1m (1⅛yd). Each new section of gathering threads should overlap the previous section by about 2.5cm (1in).

TIP

ZIGZAG METHOD

To gather over a long distance, or with a heavy fabric, lay a fine cord or top stitching thread along the edge to be gathered, and work zigzag stitch over it. Then pull up the thread.

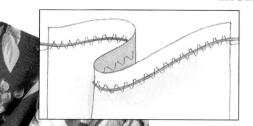

Attaching frills. . .

. . . to straight edges or curves

1 **Positioning frill** With right sides together and raw edges aligned, pin the frill to the fabric, matching markers on frill to the item.

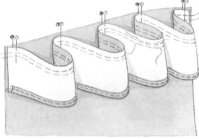

2 **Drawing up gathering** Pick up both bobbin threads and, holding the fabric lightly with your other hand, gently pull them until the frill fits. Adjust the gathers so that they are even.

3 **Stitching** Tack the frill in place, then machine stitch between the two rows of gathering. Remove gathering threads. Trim the seam to reduce bulk and neaten the raw seam edges with zigzag stitch or binding.

4 **Optional top stitching** To help the frill sit flat, press seams towards the item. Top stitch on right side, 6mm (¼in) in from seam, catching seam allowances down at same time.

TIP

RUFFLER FOOT
You can get a special ruffler attachment for machines, which will do the gathering for you, but remember to measure a test strip before and after stitching to work out the length of fabric needed.

. . . to right-angled corners

Attach frill as before, allowing extra fullness at the corners so that the frill will sit flat. Clip into the frill seam allowance at each corner.

. . . between two layers of fabric

Pin then tack the frill in place as before. Position the second layer of fabric on top, right sides together, and tack in place. Stitch the seam through all three layers of fabric. Finally trim seam to reduce bulk and turn the item to the right side.

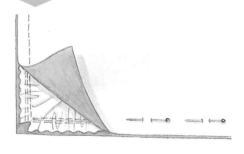

Frill variations

Folded frills
A folded frill is cut in a double thickness of fabric, with the folded edge creating a neat outer edge for the finished frill. Folded frills can be layered, provided they are made in a lightweight fabric such as chintz. Using a folded layer eliminates the need for a hem and the frill looks good from both sides.
To make a folded frill Cut double the required width plus twice the top seam allowance. Join lengths together, if necessary, as for a single frill. To neaten frill ends, fold frill in half lengthways, right sides together, and stitch across the ends. Clip across corners and turn frill to right side, matching then tacking raw edges together.
To trim a circular or square shape, join the strips into a ring before folding in half lengthwise. Press. Proceed with marking and gathering as for a single frill.

Shaping frill ends
When trimming a straight edge, the frill ends can be shaped or tapered. On single frills, cut the ends into a curve before hemming. On double frills, fold the frill in half lengthways, cut the end into a curve then stitch it.

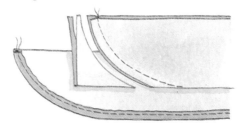

Layered frills
For the best effect make layered frills in two different coloured fabrics – perhaps the main fabric plus a contrast. They can be made with single or folded frills.
To make a layered frill Cut out and hem two frills as before, with the second (top) frill slightly narrower than the first. Match the raw edges of the two frills together and then proceed with gathering and attaching as for a single frill.
For a lacy frill, choose lace narrower than the frill and pin the lace to the frill before gathering.

Trims
Bound edge Neaten one raw edge of the frill length with a contrasting bias binding before making up the frill.
Piping cord This can be inserted between the frill and the fabric – attach the piping before the frill.

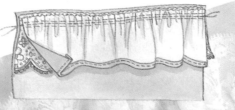

One of the fundamentals of any home sewing project, a well finished seam gives a professional look to soft furnishings.

A seam joins together two or more layers of fabric. The choice of seam, and how the seam allowances are finished, depends on the type and weight of the fabric and its end use.

The most commonly used seam is a plain one with the seam allowances either pressed open or to one side. This plain seam is suitable for items where the seam will not show, such as lined curtains or cushions.

On items where seams will be seen, such as unlined curtains or sheer fabric, use enclosed seams. These seams are strong, give a neat finish and are not difficult to do. For the best results on all seams, press them at each stage, working the point of the iron into the seam so that it sits completely flat.

Stitching a plain straight seam

A plain seam has a row of stitches running parallel to the seam edge for its entire length. Before sewing, make sure the raw seam edges are lined up correctly, and tack or pin the fabric to hold it in place while sewing. A straight stitch is used for most seams; for stretch fabrics set the machine to a small zigzag stitch.

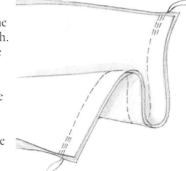

To secure the seam, stitch 1cm (⅜in) along the seam, reverse stitch direction to stitch back, then continue stitching forwards. Use the seam guidelines etched into the machine plate to keep stitching in a straight line. Complete the seam by backstitching 1cm (⅜in). Press the seam allowance open or to one side.

Finishes for pressed open seams

Pinked Use pinking shears to cut a pinked edge on light to heavyweight fabrics that won't fray at all (felts, vinyls) or fray only slightly (tightly woven cottons). This method isn't suitable for items that need frequent laundering. Pinking shears are sold in fabric departments.

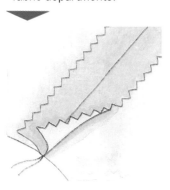

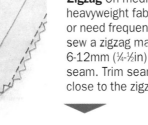

Stitched and pinked To make a pinked seam sturdier, machine stitch about 3mm (⅛in) from the pinked edge. These seams will not withstand frequent laundering.

Zigzag On medium to heavyweight fabrics that fray or need frequent washing, sew a zigzag machine stitch 6-12mm (¼-½in) out from the seam. Trim seam allowance close to the zigzag stitching.

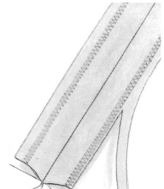

Turned and stitched For a neat, strong finish turn the edge of the seam allowance under by 3mm (⅛in) or if fabric frays a lot 6mm (¼in). Press and then stitch along edge of fold. This method is ideal for light or soft fabrics, where a zigzag finish may show through on right side.

Stitching curved seams

Set the machine to small straight stitch and stitch slowly to achieve a smooth curve. Curved seams allowances need to be clipped, so that they sit flat.

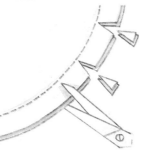

Inward curves Clip V shapes out of seam allowances. Clipping reduces bulk when the seam cannot be pressed open, as on a circular cushion. Pink or zigzag stitch allowances if necessary.

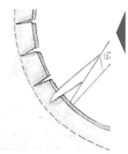

Outward curves Cut slits into the seam allowances, holding the scissors just short of seam line to avoid cutting through stitching. Pink or zigzag stitch the allowances if necessary.

Stitching corners

The key to stitching around a corner is to pivot the fabric at exactly the point where the two seams meet.

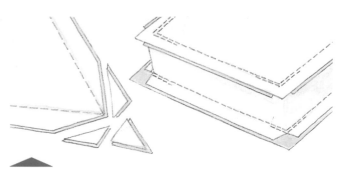

Sewing round a corner
Tack the seam if inexperienced or pin it to mark the cross point. Stitch up to the cross point, lift the machine foot up leaving the needle in place. Pivot the fabric on the needle, lower the foot and continue to stitch along the adjacent seam.

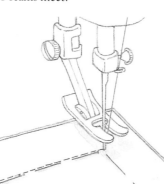

Trimming corners Trim across the corners of the seam allowance to reduce bulk, cutting across the point close to the stitching. If the corner is very sharp, taper back the sides as well. To turn the corner on a welted or boxed cushion, clip into the welt at the corner point and reinforce the corner with an extra row of stitching.

Self-enclosed seams

With these seams all the seam allowances are enclosed within the finished seam. They give a hardwearing, neat seam that is suitable for many fabrics and when the seam will be seen.

Flat fell seam

A flat fell seam is perfect for home furnishings which need to stand up to frequent washing and general wear and tear. It suits medium to heavyweight fabrics. One row of straight stitching will show on the right side.

1 **Stitching** Sew a straight seam. Trim the underneath seam allowance to 6mm (¼in) and press the allowances to one side.

2 **Neatening** Fold the top allowance over the underneath allowance, turning under the raw edge to enclose the trimmed edge. Pin and press flat. Tack then sew through all the layers close to the folded edge. Press well.

French seam

A French seam is stitched twice, once from the right side of the fabric and once from the wrong side. It is ideal for sheers and lightweight fabrics, but medium and heavyweight fabrics would make it too bulky.

1 **Stitching** With wrong sides together sew a narrow seam at least 1cm (⅜in) from seam line. Trim the seam allowances to within 3mm (⅛in) of the stitching line.

2 **Neatening** Fold fabric along the machined edge so right sides are together. Press well. Stitch along the seam line, which will enclose the raw edges of the seam allowance. Press seam to one side.

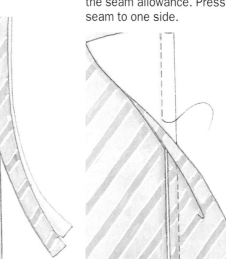

Lapped seam

A lapped seam is used to match patterns on fabric and to join bulky widths of interlining.

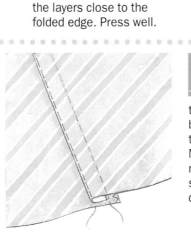

1 **Stitching** First neaten raw edges with zigzag stitch. Turn under one edge by 6mm (¼in) and pin then tack in place over the other piece to be joined. On patterned fabrics, adjust the layers to match the pattern. Machine stitch along the fold on the right side of the fabric. Sew another seam parallel to the first to catch down the raw edge underneath.

2 **To finish** Remove the tacking. Press the seam flat with a warm iron.

Gathered Valance (Skirt)

Personalize your bedroom with a gathered bed valance (skirt).
In colours that team with a selection of bedlinen, and cut to the
fullness and depth of your choice, it can soften any room.

The sweep of fabric in a gathered bed valance provides a softening touch for your bedroom, concealing the bed base and legs, and the space under the bed so often used for storage. Marry the colours of the valance with the colours featured elsewhere in the bedroom, in curtains or on wallpaper borders. Try to choose colours that also work with the

sheets, pillowcases and duvet covers you use on your bed.

Use light or mediumweight furnishing fabrics to make the valance. Since only the frill is visible, you can make the central panel from an old sheet or lining fabric. An even more economical alternative is to simply attach the frill to a band of fabric that can easily be tucked beneath the mattress.

The crisp bright colours of a full skirted bed valance are accented with a binding trim stitched around the frill hem. A fine line of piping, fitted between the central panel and frill, completes the tailored finish.

MAKING A BED VALANCE

YOU WILL NEED

❖ FABRIC (see below for amounts)

❖ SEWING THREAD

❖ TAPE MEASURE

❖ SCISSORS

❖ PINS

A bed valance is made to fit neatly over the bed base, with a decorative skirt hanging over the foot and down on either side. If the central panel is made from a cheaper fabric or from an old sheet, and its edge is visible, you may wish hide it. One way of doing this is to stitch a narrow strip of the frill fabric round the edges of the central panel, before attaching the frill.

To ensure that the valance skirt looks full when using lighter weight fabrics, allow more fabric for the frill.

FABRIC AMOUNTS

For the central panel, measure the length and width of the bed base, adding 4.5cm (1¾in) to the length and 3cm (1¼in) to the width for the hem and seam allowances.

For the frill, the drop should equal the distance from the top of the bed base to the floor, plus 6.5cm (2½in). The length depends on the fullness of the frill, but as a general rule, it should be one and a half to twice the length that the frill must cover – both sides of the bed plus the end of it. The drop of a standard valance is 30-35cm (12-13¾in), but check the height of your own bed base.

◀ *Making up the curtains and a bed valance in the same fabric creates a smartly tailored look for this room. The vertical stripes give the bed extra stature.*

1 Cutting out the fabric Use the measurements in Fabric Amounts, above, to cut a central panel the size of the bed base, joining widths of fabric if necessary. For the frill cut strips across the width of the fabric, unless you wish to make a feature of a directional pattern.

2 Preparing the central panel Turn up a 2.5cm (1in) double hem along one short edge of the central panel, pin and stitch.

4 Sectioning the fabric Measure the length of the frill and divide it into six to eight equal sections, marking with pins or coloured tacking stitches. Measure the sides and the raw edge of the central panel and divide by the number of sections of your frill. Mark the sections on the central panel.

3 Preparing the frill Join the frill pieces into one long strip using french seams. Take care to match the pattern direction on all the pieces. Turn under a 2.5cm (1in) double hem on lower and side edges of the frill and machine stitch.

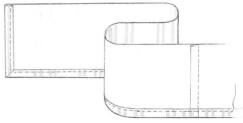

5 Stitching the gathering Run two parallel rows of gathering stitches 1.2cm (½in) and 2cm (¾in) in from the raw edge of the frill. To make drawing up the threads easier, stop and start the stitching at the section marks.

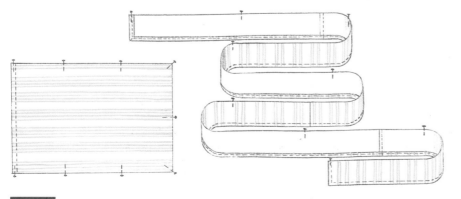

6 **Attaching the frill** With right sides together and raw edges even, pin the frill to the central panel, matching the marks. Pull up the gathering stitches to fit. Arrange gathers evenly down both sides, but pull them slightly tighter at the corners to allow extra fabric for ease.

7 **Stitching the frill** Tack and stitch the frill in place between the rows of gathering stitches. Clip into the seam allowance at the frill corners. Trim seam allowances and neaten the raw edge with binding or zigzag stitch. Press seam toward frill.

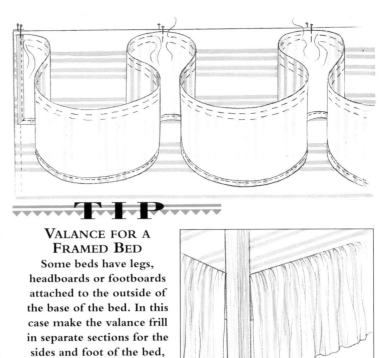

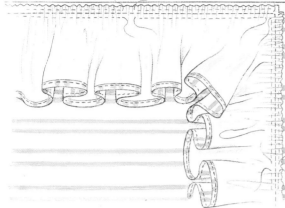

TIP

VALANCE FOR A FRAMED BED

Some beds have legs, headboards or footboards attached to the outside of the base of the bed. In this case make the valance frill in separate sections for the sides and foot of the bed, so that they hang around the bed frame.

◀ *A triple layered frill, sewn together and gathered as one piece, ties in with the patchwork of colours in the quilt and the ruched window dressing.*

MAKING A TUCK-IN BED VALANCE

To help reduce the amount of fabric that is required, especially in the case of double, queen and king-size beds, consider attaching the frilled skirt to a band of fabric that is tucked between the bed base and the mattress, rather than attaching it to a full central panel.

1 Cutting out the frill
Use the measurements in Fabric Amounts, on the previous page, to cut strips of fabric for the frill. Cut all the pieces across the width of the fabric.

2 Cutting out the band
First measure the sides and the foot of the bed. Then cut out two strips of fabric the length of the bed sides, plus 4.5cm (1¾in), by 30cm (12in) wide. Cut out one strip of fabric the length of the foot end, plus 3cm (1¼in), by 30cm (12in) wide.

A simple, short skirted valance emphasizes the stately height and elegance of this wrought iron bed while effectively hiding the bed base.

3 Cutting the mitres
Fold both short edges of the end strip diagonally, so that they are level with the long edge. Cut along the fold. Deal with one short edge of the side strips in the same way.

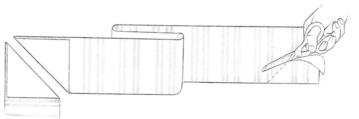

4 Joining the mitres
With the right sides facing, carefully pin the mitred corners of the side strips to the mitred corners of the end strip. Then stitch the corners together to within 1.5cm (⅝in) of the inner seam.

5 Hemming band Along the inner edge of the band, turn under and stitch a 1.5cm (⅝in) double hem, allowing the mitred corner seams to part. At the ends of the band turn under and stitch a 1.5cm (⅝in) double hem.

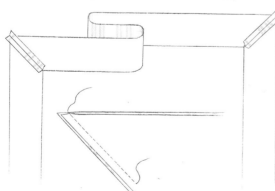

6 Making up the valance Prepare and attach the frill as in steps 3-7 on the previous page. Fit on the bed, tucking the band between the base and mattress.

QUILTED VALANCE (SKIRT)

The geometric lines of a fitted bed valance (skirt) are subtly softened with light padding and rows of quilting. Its neat, streamlined look makes it an ideal choice for a contemporary bedroom.

A fitted bed valance (skirt) is a smartly tailored way to hide the base and legs of a divan bed. It's made in a similar way to a gathered valance – the quilted skirt is attached to a central panel that sits on top of the bed base – with the advantage that it uses less fabric than the gathered version.

Padding and quilting the valance skirt gives body and substance to the fabric, so that it holds its shape and retains a trim, fitted look. As the skirt is cut from a narrow panel of fabric it is relatively easy to quilt – the complete width of the panel fits under the arm of the machine.

Although you can quilt the skirt in any design, the easiest option is to quilt it in straight rows. Working with a striped or checked fabric makes quilting even easier, as the pattern of the fabric provides the stitching guidelines. If you use a plain fabric or one in another pattern, you need to mark on the stitching lines.

For the main fabric, a mediumweight, closely woven fabric is the best choice. To cut costs, use an old sheet or inexpensive backing fabric for the central panel and to back the valance. Use polyester wadding for the padding – it's washable and easy to work with.

Checked or striped fabrics provide ready stitching guides for quilting in straight rows. Before you buy a patterned fabric, it's important to decide on the direction of the pattern – whether it will run around the bed, or down the depth of the valance.

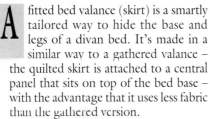

Read more on quilting on pages 13-14.

MAKING THE VALANCE

YOU WILL NEED

❖ FURNISHING FABRIC
❖ WADDING – lightweight 50g (2oz)
❖ BACKING FABRIC
❖ SEWING THREAD
❖ TAPE MEASURE

The valance consists of padding sandwiched between two layers of fabric – a backing and the main fabric. To allow for shrinkage due to quilting, cut the valance skirt panel 10cm (4in) larger than the final measurements and trim it to size after it has been quilted.

FABRIC AMOUNTS

Measure the bed and work out the fabric requirements before you buy the fabric. It's best to cut the valance panels down the length of the fabric. It takes slightly more fabric than cutting them across the width, but avoids too many joins. If you wish to make a feature of a directional pattern, or the fabric is very expensive, you can cut the panels across the fabric width.

As a rough guide to the amount of main fabric and wadding for a standard double bed, cutting the panels along the fabric length, allow the length of the bed plus one-and-a-half times its width, about 4m (4⅓yd). You need the same amount of backing, plus enough to cover the bed base.

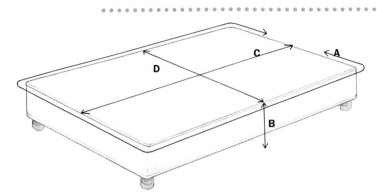

1 Cutting out the valance skirt Measure around the sides and lower end of base and add 24cm (9½in) so skirt wraps around at head end (**A**). Measure from the top of the bed base to the desired skirt drop (**B**). Add 13cm (5⅛in) to both measurements for seams and shrinkage due to quilting. Cut strips of main fabric to these measurements, adding 3cm (1¼in) for each join and extra for pattern matching. Join strips taking 1.5cm (⅝in) seams. Press seams open. Cut and join strips of backing fabric to the same size. Cut strips of wadding to the same size and butt join with herringbone stitch.

2 Tacking the wadding Using tailors' chalk, mark quilting lines on the right side of the main fabric (optional). Lay the fabric right side down on a flat surface and pin the wadding on top. Starting at the centre and working outwards, tack the layers together in rows – placed about 20cm (8in) apart – across the width of the skirt. Then tack around the outer edges as well.

3 Adding the skirt backing With the right sides together, pin and then stitch together the backing and the main fabric (wadding attached) at each short end and along the hem. Clip the corners and turn to the right side so that the wadding is sandwiched between the fabric. Press thoroughly. Tack all three layers together along both the centre and the top edge.

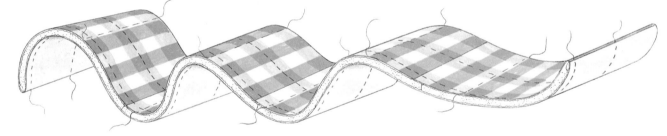

4 Quilting the fabric Check the sewing machine tension on a scrap of fabric and wadding. Adjust it if necessary. To support the quilting while you are sewing, fold it into concertina pleats and rest it on your lap. Stitching the row closest to the seamed edge first, machine quilt rows along the length of the skirt. Trim the quilted layers along the top raw edge to measure depth **B**, plus 1.5cm (⅝in) for seams. Remove the tacking stitches.

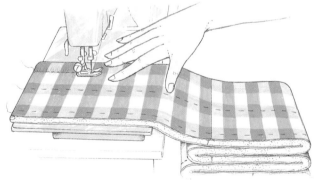

5 Adding the central panel Measure length (**C**) and width (**D**) of base. Add 4.5cm (1¾in) to the length and 3cm (1¼in) to the width. Cut a rectangle of backing fabric to this size. Stitch a double 1.5cm (⅝in) hem along one short edge. With right sides together and raw edges even, pin skirt to panel so the ends of skirt extend around bed head. Machine stitch, clip corners and neaten seam. Fit valance over bed base.

BED CORONETS

Formal bed coronets look impressive,
yet are simply lined curtains suspended from a special
shaped track fitted above the bed.

An attractive coronet of fabric that sits high above the bed and sweeps down in graceful folds turns a plain bedroom into a romantic haven. The coronet can be as simple as an ordinary pair of curtains, or become a more elaborate affair with the addition of a frilled and piped valance.

Any fabric that can be used in curtain making is suitable for bed coronets, so you can choose to mix or match with the window treatment. The back curtain and lining of the side curtains can blend or contrast with the main curtaining – try a smaller print, or a plain or striped fabric, to complete the look.

Fit for a princess – a bed coronet must be every little girl's idea of a dream bedroom. The choice of vivid striped fabric here ensures that the final look is not over fussy.

MAKING THE CORONET

The instructions on these pages show how to make a coronet based on a kit track with curtains to frame a standard double bed. The kit comes complete with brackets for putting up the track, which is fitted with gliders to carry the curtain hooks. The valance is fitted to the top of the track, in front of the curtains, with special valance clips. If you have trouble finding a suitable kit, instructions are given overpage for making a coronet shelf from inexpensive board.

These coronet drapes consist of three separate curtains – two side curtains and a back curtain. The side ones need to be lined, but to save cost, the back curtain can be made of lining fabric alone, to match the lining of the curtains. The valance, which is just a very short curtain, is made separately. Here it is lined, with a frill inserted between the lining and the main fabric.

The headings on the coronet curtains and valance need to be gathered up with a heading tape – standard gathered tape is used here, but any style is suitable. On the valance the tape is positioned to form a frilled heading.

Look for coronet kits and curtain fittings in department stores and specialist shops.

YOU WILL NEED

❖ CORONET TRACK
❖ TWO TIEBACK HOOKS
❖ FABRIC for SIDE CURTAINS and VALANCE
❖ LINING for CURTAINS and VALANCE
❖ PLAIN FABRIC for BINDING, PIPING CORD
❖ THREAD, HEADING TAPE, CURTAIN HOOKS
❖ VALANCE CLIPS

PREPARATION AND MEASURING UP

1 Fixing up the track Mark the height of the coronet above the bed – coronets are often placed 220cm (7ft) above a bed. Following maker's instructions, fix the track at the marked point. Fit a tieback hook on each side of the bed.

2 Measuring back curtain Allow one standard 122cm (48in) width of lining fabric for the back curtain. For the length, measure from the back of the track to the floor and add 6.5cm (2⅝in) for hem and heading.

3 Measuring for side curtains To work out the length of the side curtains, tie string to the track and drape it down behind the tieback hook to the floor. Note the length and add 3cm (1¼in) for hem and heading. Each side curtain is made up of one and a half fabric widths, so allow three times the final length. Allow for the same amount of lining.

4 Measuring a valance Measure from the track to the chosen length – valances are usually between 30-50cm (12-20in) deep. Deduct the depth of the frilled edge and then add 20cm (8in) for hem and heading frill. Allow for two fabric widths, and an extra 30cm (12in) for the frill. Allow one curtain length in a plain fabric for binding the leading edges of the side curtains and covering piping cord on valance.

◀ *The choice of a floral fabric lined with a coordinating check keeps these bed drapes looking fresh and modern.*

1 **Making back curtain** Turn under a double 1cm (⅜in) hem down both sides; pin and machine stitch. Turn up a double 2.5cm (1in) base hem; pin and machine stitch. Turn down top edge for 1.5cm (⅝in) and stitch heading tape to cover raw edge. Gather tape so it's taut across back of track. Secure with a hook at each end of tape slotted into endstops.

2 **Cutting out side curtain** Cut out three fabric widths to the final length from step 3, *Preparation*. Fold one width in half lengthways matching selvedges. Carefully cut down the fold. Pin and machine stitch one half width to outside edges of both full widths to form each curtain. Repeat to make two lining panels of the same size.

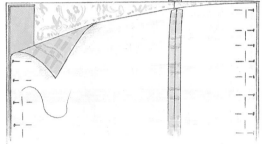

3 **Making the side curtains** To insert binding along curtain front edge, cut plain fabric to the curtain length, by 8cm (3¼in) wide. Fold in half with wrong sides together, matching raw edges. Position to right side of main curtain fabric, matching raw edges. Place lining to main fabric with right sides together. Pin, tack and machine stitch the side and base edges taking 1.5cm (⅝in) seams. Trim and turn right side out. Repeat with second curtain.

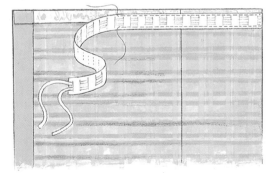

4 **Forming top heading** Treating main fabric and lining as one, turn down top edge for 1.5cm (⅝in). Stitch heading tape to cover raw edges. Gather tape so each curtain fits half of track. Put hooks into heading tape and hang curtains on gliders to meet in the centre front.

5 **Cutting out valance** Cut fabric and lining to measurements from step 4, *Preparation*. For frill, measure hem edge and allow 1½ times length. Decide on frill depth – about 6cm (2¼in) – adding 3.5cm (1¼in) for hem and seams.

6 **Inserting the piping** Cut a length of piping cord the same length as the valance hem and cover with plain contrasting fabric. Neaten ends of piping. Tack firmly along base edge of valance with cord facing inward and raw edges together.

7 **Gathering the frill** Turn under a double 1cm (⅜in) hem along base and sides of frill; pin and machine stitch. Work two rows of gathering stitches along top of frill. Pin at intervals to valance hem over piping, gathering up evenly to fit, and tack. Place lining to valance with right sides together. Pin and stitch edges and hem together. Trim and turn right side out.

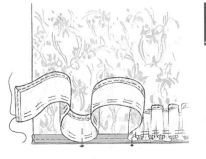

◤ *If the bed is pushed up against a wall like this, two coronet curtains provide an effective frame when draped over head and foot ends.*

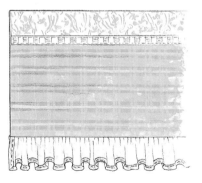

8 **Hanging the valance** Treating the main fabric and lining as one, turn back 8cm (3¼in) hem on top edge of valance and tack. Position the heading tape so that it covers the raw edges and stitch it in place. Gather up the heading to fit the track and use the valance clips to hang the valance in front of the side curtains.

MAKING A CORONET SHELF

YOU WILL NEED

- ❖ 20mm (¾in) thick PLYWOOD measuring 50 x 30cm (20 x 12in)
- ❖ TWO METAL ANGLE BRACKETS with SCREWS and WALLPLUGS
- ❖ STRING, NAIL, HAMMER, PENCIL
- ❖ JIGSAW, SANDPAPER
- ❖ CURTAIN FABRIC, 50 x 35cm (20 x 13¾in)
- ❖ STAPLE GUN and STAPLES
- ❖ HEADING TAPE and DOUBLE-SIDED TAPE

Without a specialist track you will need to make a coronet shelf from blockboard and fix it above the bed on angle brackets. In this case, two side curtains are simply held in place on the shelf by heading tape against double-sided tape, available from department stores and specialist shops. To estimate the amount of fabric and lining you need, follow step 3, *Preparation and Measuring up* on the previous page. Allow extra to cover the shelf.

1 Cutting out the coronet shelf
Hammer a nail into the centre of one long edge of the board. Tie one end of the string around the nail and the other around the pencil so that when the string is taut it measures 22cm (8¾in). Keeping the string taut, draw a semicircle. Using the jigsaw, cut out the shelf. Sand the edges smooth. Screw the angle brackets to the underside of the shelf.

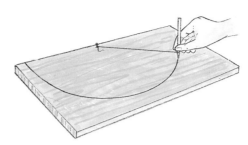

2 Covering the coronet shelf Lay the blockboard on the wrong side of the fabric and mark round. Cut out, adding 4cm (1½in) all round. Wrap the fabric edges over the top of the coronet shelf, snipping into fabric so it will lie flat and sit round the brackets; staple the edges down.

3 Fixing the double-sided tape Stick the self-adhesive, double-sided tape round the curved front edge of the coronet shelf to hold the curtains when the heading tape is pushed against it.
Using wallplugs and screws, fix the coronet shelf securely to the wall.

4 Making side curtains Make up each side curtain as given on previous page, but in place of standard tape, stitch on the heading tape. Handstitch centre front leading edges of curtains together for 10cm (4in). Pull up the heading tape evenly on the curtains and press in place over the tape round the edge of the coronet shelf.

☑ *A coronet shelf is a completely invisible way of hanging simple curtains symmetrically over an ornamental bedhead.*

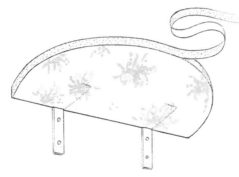

ADDING A VALANCE

To add a valance using this method, insert screw eyes into the underside of the shelf. Make the side curtains with standard heading tape and hang them up using curtain hooks passed through the screw eyes. Attach the valance to the edge of the shelf with heading tape.

Inserting screw eyes Drive the screw eyes into the underside of the blockboard round the curved edge, spacing them approximately 6cm (2½in) apart.

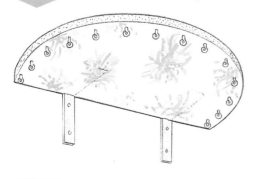

CUSHION BEDHEADS

Cushions suspended from a curtain pole provide extra comfort and an attractive headrest for a divan bed. Hanging along the length of a bed, they also create an instant and economical sofa.

A covered cushion or pillow hanging from a curtain pole is a comfortable addition to a bed without a headboard. The cushions hang from the pole, attached either by ties or tabs, or by a casing stitched to the back of the cushion cover so that it sits in front of the curtain pole. Ideally the pole should be positioned on the wall so that the cushions create a comfortable back and headrest when you are sitting up in bed. You can hide the pole, or you can turn it into a feature by extending the ends on either side of the cushions and adding decorative finials.

Covered cushions are also an excellent way of turning a spare bed into a sofa. Simply push the bed lengthways against the wall and hang one large or several shorter cushions along the wall.

Threaded on a reed-thin rod this pretty, frilled bedhead is padded with a spare pillow. Echo the crisp floral fabric by making up the curtains in the same design.

43

CUSHION BEDHEAD WITH TIES

Foam pads are used as the base for these cushions. Buy 7.5cm (3in) thick foam from a specialist supplier, who can cut it to size. For the cushion cover use a mediumweight cotton furnishing fabric. The cushion is suspended from three sets of ties, sewn into the upper edge of the cover and tied in bows around the fitted curtain pole. Instructions are given for one cushion; for a double bed make two cushions and hang them side by side.

MEASURING UP

1 **Measuring for the pole** Measure the width of the bed and, if you wish, add extra length for the curtain pole to extend beyond the bed width. Purchase a curtain pole up to this length.

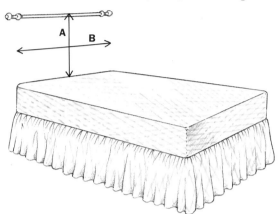

2 **Fixing the pole** Mark the height of the curtain pole above the bed. Gauge this by sitting up in the bed; for comfort the pole should be positioned above the top of your head. Following the manufacturer's instructions, fix the curtain pole at the marked position.

3 **Measuring for the foam pads** Decide on the number of cushions – two look better on a double bed. Measure from top of pole to the desired height above the bed (**A**) and deduct 5cm (2in) for hanging ties. Measure the bed's width (**B**) – for two cushions halve **B**, with a small gap between cushions. Cut foam pad to **A** less 5cm (2in) x **B** (or ½**B**).

YOU WILL NEED
❖ TAPE MEASURE
❖ CURTAIN POLE, SUPPORTS and FINIALS
❖ FOAM – 7.5cm (3in) thick
❖ COTTON FURNISHING FABRIC
❖ ZIP – 5cm (2in) less than pad depth (width)
❖ MATCHING THREAD

▶ *A pair of cushion bedheads hung side by side is the best choice for a double bed. The white wooden pole extends past the cushions for extra elegance.*

MAKING THE CUSHION BEDHEAD

1 **Cutting out the cover** Measure around the cushion pad (**C**) and add a 3cm (1¼in) seam allowance. Measure the depth of the pad (**D**) and add 10.5cm (4¼in) for gussets and seam allowances. Cut out one piece of furnishing fabric to these measurements.

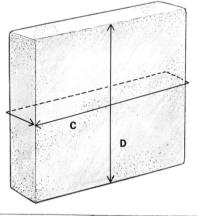

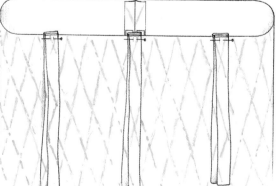

2 **Making up the cover** With right sides together, fold cover fabric in half widthways. Pin and tack a 1.5cm (⅝in) seam. Machine stitch seam for 8cm (3¼in) from each edge and press seam open. Centre the zip face down on the wrong side of seam. Pin, tack and stitch zip into place from the right side.

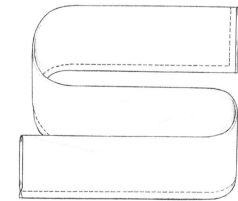

3 **Making the ties** Cut six strips 50 x 11cm (20 x 4¼in). Fold strips in half lengthways, right sides together. Pin, stitch the long and one short edge. Trim, turn right side out and press. In pairs, match edges, pin and tack.

4 **Placing the ties** Centre zip at back of cover and open it. Mark positions of the ties on the top front edge of cover – one pair 7.5cm (3in) from each side edge and the remaining pair centrally between the two. Matching raw edges, pin ties to the right side of the front cover at marked positions. Turn cover to wrong side and machine stitch a 1.5cm (⅝in) seam along top edge, catching in ties. Stitch lower edge. Turn cover to right side through zip opening.

5 **Adding the pad** Insert pad through zip opening. Tuck excess fabric at corners under seam to form a neat V-shape. Slipstitch to secure.

6 **Hanging the cushions** Pin the ties in position around the curtain pole so the cushion is level. One at a time, unpin each pair of ties and tie a firm bow.

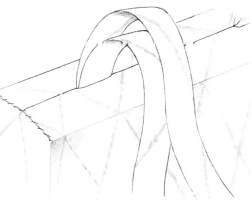

TIP

INNER COVER
To prolong the life of the cushion, you may wish to make a calico inner cover for the foam pad. Make up in the same way as the cushion cover omitting the zip and the ties. Leave one end of the calico cover open, insert the pad, fold edges under and slipstitch in place.

FRILLED CUSHION BEDHEAD

YOU WILL NEED

❖ FURNISHING FABRIC
❖ PILLOW
❖ FINE CURTAIN ROD AND FIXTURES
❖ MATCHING SEWING THREAD

You can make soft hanging bedheads very simply using pillows. In this case a fine curtain rod slides through a casing topstitched across the back of the cover, so that the pillow hangs in front of the rod. Alternatively, fit loops or ties into the upper seam to hang the cushion below a curtain pole. Fix the curtain rod to the wall, adjusting the height to suit the method of hanging.

▶ See pages 29-30 for adding frills, and pages 93-94 for making pillow pads.

1 Measuring up Measure the width and length of the pillow and cut out two pieces of furnishing fabric to these measurements plus 1.5cm (⅝in) seam allowances all round.

2 Adding a frill Measure all round one pillow piece and double the measurement. Cut a piece of fabric this length by 20cm (8in) wide. With right sides together, stitch the frill strip into a ring, press seams open. Fold frill in half lengthways, wrong sides together. Work two rows of gathering stitches along raw edges. Pulling up gathering to fit, pin frill to right side of front pillow piece. Tack and machine stitch.

3 Stitching casing to back Cut a casing as long as the pillow and approximately 8cm (3¼in) wide – check that the casing is wide enough to take the curtain rod. Press under 1.5cm (⅝in) hem on long edges. Press and stitch a 2cm (¾in) hem on each end. Position casing 5cm (2in) down from top edge of back pillow piece, with wrong side of casing to right side of pillow piece. Pin and topstitch long edges.

4 Making up cover Place front and back pillow pieces together with right sides together. Pin and stitch all round leaving a 30cm (12in) opening centrally on one short side. Take care not to stitch across casing ends. Clip corners to seam allowance and turn right side out. Insert pillow and slipstitch opening closed. Slide the curtain rod through casing and hang above the bed.

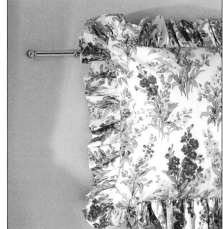

▲ *A deep double frill adds feminine charm to a soft pillow bedhead.*

▼ *Fun stripes and a hand carved finial make a really special feature for a child's bedroom.*

BEDHEADS WITH TABS

Gusseted cushions make a firm, comfortable back and headrest for a bed. Their chunky geometrical shape works particularly well with neat tabs – make two or three tabs for hanging each cushion.

Here the natural colours and texture of the fabric are complemented by using a wooden curtain rail and wooden button details at the points of the tabs.

For each tab cut two strips of fabric 10 x 30cm (4 x 12in). Place them in pairs, with right sides together. Sew the strips on long edges and to a point in the middle on one short edge. Trim, turn to the right side and press for a neat finish.

Make a piped gusseted cushion, sewing the raw edges of the tabs between the back panel and the gusset on the top back edge. Sew a button on the pointed end and, ifnally, handstitch this to the front of the completed cushion.

BED CANOPIES

Simple bed canopies, made from two unlined curtain widths,
echo the attractive curves of window drapes and provide the opportunity
to display more of a favourite fabric.

A softly draping canopy over a bed or baby's crib is a graceful feature. There are two ways of making a bed canopy – you can either make one with a casing (or stitched tube) that slips over a short length of ordinary curtain pole, or you can use a canopy kit. If you opt for a kit, you can use curtains with casings or you can hang ready-made curtains on the kit rod using special curtain hooks.

Any lightweight curtain fabric that drapes well is suitable for a bed canopy. You can line the curtains with a contrasting fabric for extra visual interest, if you wish, but canopies work perfectly well without a lining, provided you choose a fabric that looks good on both sides. Sheer fabrics, such as lace, voile or muslin, also make effective canopies – their soft and filmy nature is ideal for a romantic bedroom or baby's crib.

A frill or braid trim stitched on to the front and lower edges of the canopy adds the perfect finishing touch. To hold the curtains off the bed, you can drape them back on either side with tiebacks or holdbacks. Or you can simply allow the canopy to sweep freely to the floor.

For a glamorous day-bed, position the bed against a wall and drape the canopy along its length. Draping the canopy in this way shows off its decorative lining to perfection.

47

MAKING A BED CANOPY

You can use any type of curtain pole for hanging the canopy, provided you can trim it to size first and fix it at right angles to the wall above your bed. Buy a decorative finial to cap the end of the pole so the canopy doesn't slip off.

The width of the canopy curtain should be about two and a half times the length of the curtain pole. In practice, it's best to simply use the width of the fabric as the curtain width. The instructions below are for an unlined canopy.

You can make the canopy with or without a stand-up frilled heading above the curtain pole. This gives a softer finish to the look – for a doubly feminine effect, team it with a frill down the front edges.

▶ *Twin canopies, made in the same blue and yellow fabric as the duvet covers, are a stylish addition to the beds in this guest room. In this case a kit track supports the curtains which are made with a casing.*

YOU WILL NEED

- ❖ CURTAIN POLE, trimmed to 45cm (18in)
- ❖ WALL FIXINGS
- ❖ FINIAL
- ❖ CURTAIN FABRIC
- ❖ MATCHING SEWING THREAD
- ❖ BALL OF STRING
- ❖ TAPE MEASURE
- ❖ DRILL AND DRILL BITS

1 Fitting the pole Decide on the best height for the curtain pole – usually about 1.85-2m (6ft-6ft 6in) above the top of the mattress. Fix the pole centrally above the bed.

2 Measuring up Tie the end of the ball of string to the middle of the curtain pole and let the string drape down to the floor on one side of the bed. If you intend to have tiebacks, use a pencil to mark their position on either side of the bed. Let the string drape to the point where you want to place the tieback, hold it with your finger at this point then let it drop to the floor.

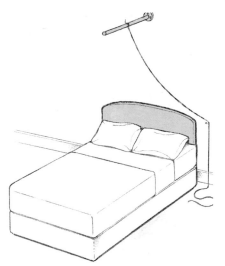

3 Cutting out Measure the string from the pole top to the floor. Add 3cm (1¼in) for the top seam and casing ease, plus 4cm (1½in) for a frill, and 10cm (4in) for the base hem. Cut two fabric widths to this length.

4 Stitching the canopy Place the two canopy pieces with right sides together and raw edges even, making sure that the pattern on both pieces runs up the fabric. Pin and stitch the top edges, taking a 1.5cm (⅝in) seam allowance. Press the seam open. Turn under and pin a double 1cm (⅜in) hem along each long edge of the canopy. Turn under and pin a double 5cm (2in) base hem at each end. Mitre the base corners neatly. Stitch the side and base hems.

5 Measuring for the casing Measure the circumference of the curtain pole and divide the measurement in half. Add 1.5cm (⅝in) to this measurement for ease. This is the width of the casing.

6 Stitching the casing With the *wrong* sides together, fold the canopy along the centre seam. To make a frilled heading above the casing, pin both layers of fabric together 4cm (1½in) from the fold and topstitch. To make the casing, pin and stitch the required width of the casing from this seam, or from the fold if there is no frilled heading. To hang the canopy, slide the casing along the curtain pole. Attach the finial to hold the canopy in place.

QUICK BED CANOPY

You can make a no-sew bed canopy using a bed canopy kit and a pair of ready-made curtains. The kit consists of a short curtain track, wall fixings and double-sided curtain hooks, so that you can hang a curtain from each side of the track. Follow step 2 of *Making a Bed Canopy* to work out your curtain length and re-hem the curtains if necessary.

Fabric rosettes are an ideal way of disguising the end of the curtain rod and making tieback decorations. For a quick rosette, cut a strip of fabric about 60 x 20cm (24 x 8in). Turn under, pin and stitch a narrow double hem on both short edges. Fold the strip in half lengthways, right sides together, and stitch the long edges together. Turn the tube right side out.

Thread a short length of elastic through the tube, pull up both ends, knot them together and trim off the excess. Gently shape the tube into a rosette, overlapping the hemmed edges to cover the knotted elastic.

▶ *Many duvet covers and bedding ranges are sold with matching ready-made curtains – put them to inventive use as a bed canopy, using a track specially made for the purpose.*

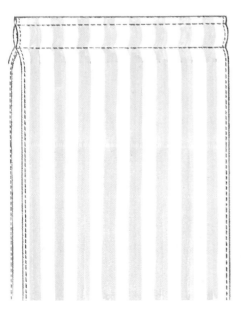

1 **Fixing the canopy rod** Decide on the best height for the canopy rod and fix it in place centrally above the bed, following the manufacturer's instructions. Clip the curtain hooks on to the rod, spacing them 5cm (2in) apart along the length.

2 **Assembling the canopy** Hang one curtain on each side of the rod, fitting the hooks into the bottom two pockets of the heading tape. Place the last hooks 4cm (1½in) from the edge of the tape. Clip the end cap on to the rod and decorate it as you wish.

DESIGN IDEAS

To liven up the bed drapes, you can either trim the edges of the curtains with braid or a frill. For the frill you can either use the same fabric as the drapes or pick out a colour from the pattern to use as a complementary edging.

Alternatively, you can make a feature of the curtain pole itself, by choosing a particularly ornate design or by capping it with a decorative finial.

▲ *Make an instant canopy by simply draping the fabric over the pole. This length of plain cream fabric, edged with black braid, teams perfectly with an elegant wrought-iron pole.*

▲ *A canopy covering the top and sides of a crib protects a snoozing baby from disturbing draughts and acts as a shade from excessive sunlight. A padded sun face as a finial adds a fun touch.*

◀ *The soft and feminine look of this frilled bed canopy perfectly complements the romantic rose design used throughout the room. The double layered frill gives it an indulgent look.*

TIE-ON HEADBOARD COVERS

*Designed simply to slip over an existing headboard,
a tie-on headboard cover is a practical way of coordinating
bedroom soft furnishings.*

W hether it hides an old headboard, improves a plain one, or is just for fun, a tie-on headboard cover is a bright solution for coordinating an exisiting headboard with other soft furnishings in the room.

Choose a firmly woven, medium or heavyweight fabric for the headboard cover. It could be a print, interesting textured weave, velvet or a lavish brocade – the choice is yours. Avoid lightweight or very heavy fabrics as these will not make up well.

If you are introducing a new fabric to the scheme be guided by the other colours in the room. Ensure that one of the colours in the new fabric repeats at least one of those already used, or opt for a plain fabric that picks up one of the colours in the scheme.

WHAT HEADBOARD?

The instructions on the following pages give alternatives – for covering a rectangular headboard or a shaped one. Both covers can be made to fit a headboard of any size. If you don't have a headboard, you could buy a plain medium density fibreboard (MDF) one – these are inexpensive and available by mail order.

A tie-on headboard cover made in the same fabric as the curtains and duvet cover completes the coordinated look of this bedroom.

RECTANGULAR TIE-ON COVER

This cover is simply a padded rectangle tied in place over the headboard. Side flaps, called plackets, hide the headboard underneath. For added interest the cover can be quilted, either in straight rows or if you feel daring in a more complicated pattern.

For queen and king size headboards you need to join fabric lengths together to make a piece that is wide enough. Allow one complete width as a central panel and join a strip to each side – side joins are less obvious than one in the centre. Try and match the pattern across the front when joining widths. The backing fabric will not be seen, so buy inexpensive fabric or use an old sheet.

FABRIC AMOUNTS

First measure the headboard: measure from the front, bottom edge of the headboard, where it meets the mattress, over the top and down to the same point on the back. Add 13cm (5⅛in) to this measurement for seams and stretching due to padding (**A**). Measure the width and add 10cm (4in) for seams and ease (**B**). Amounts below are based on fabric 140cm (54in) wide and wadding 90cm (35in) wide.

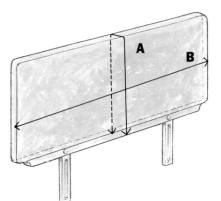

Bed size	Main fabric	Backing	Wadding
Single 91cm (3ft)	1 x A	1 x A	2 x A
Double 136cm (4ft 6in)	1½ x A	1 x A	2 x A
Queen 151cm (5ft)	2 x A	2 x A	2 x A
King 195cm (6ft 6in)	2 x A	2 x A	3 x A

▲ *The first thing to do when making a padded tie-on cover is to measure up the headboard accurately.*

1 Cutting out From the furnishing fabric, make one rectangle to the measurements **A** by **B**, joining widths as necessary and pressing seams open. For side plackets, cut two rectangles the headboard height plus 8cm (3¼in) by 20cm (8in) wide. For ties, cut 12 strips 38 x 11cm (15 x 4¼in).

From the backing fabric and wadding cut a rectangle to the measurements **A** by **B**, joining panels as necessary. To join wadding, butt the edges together and hold in position with small diagonal tacking stitches which will remain in place.

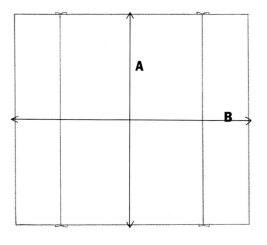

2 Hemming the side plackets Turn under and stitch a double 1cm (⅜in) hem around one long and both short edges of each side placket.

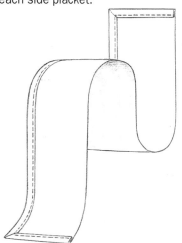

3 Stitching the ties. Fold each tie in half along its length, right sides together. Taking a 1cm (⅜in) seam, stitch across one short edge and down the long side of each tie. Clip across the corners and turn to the right side. Press.

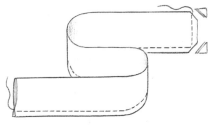

4 Adding wadding Position wadding on wrong side of main fabric. Starting from centre and working outwards, tack the two together. This tacking will be removed later.

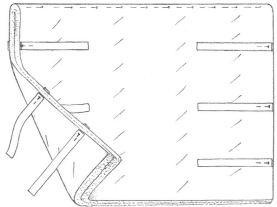

5 Adding ties With wrong sides together fold cover in half lengthways and pin along fold. Position ties to fabric right side, so that the raw ends of ties align with sides. Position three ties on each side of the front. Position ties to correspond on back section. Remove pins holding fold.

6 Adding side plackets
Position side plackets to right side of the front section of the cover over the ties. Match raw edge of each placket to the cover sides.

7 Stitching backing Position backing to right side of cover and stitch around outer edge taking a 1.5cm (⅝in) seam and leaving a large opening on one bottom edge for turning through later.

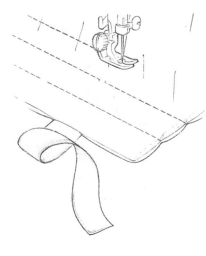

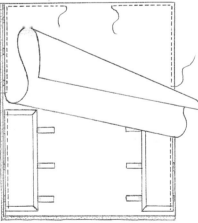

8 Finishing Trim wadding away from seams and clip across corners. Turn cover to right side and press. Stitch up opening and remove tacking. Drape cover over headboard. Tuck in side plackets to cover headboard ends and knot ties.

9 Optional quilting Machine quilt the wadding and main fabric by stitching rows parallel to sides and spaced 10cm (4in) apart. On a striped fabric use the stripes as a stitching guide for the quilting. Remove tacking after quilting.

◣ Tying a padded cover over this headboard not only matches it to the bedbase valance but also softens up the headboard itself.

TIP
DOUBLE BEDS

It will be tight to cut the double headboard cover from one length (A) of 140cm (54in) wide fabric, but it's not worth buying two lengths. If your fabric is not quite wide enough, add a band of a contrasting fabric down each side, then make the ties to match. This looks smarter – and is cheaper – than joining a small panel of the same fabric. If you choose this option, buy one length (A) of the main fabric and one length (A) of a plain fabric of any width.

SHAPED SLIP-ON COVER

Slip-on covers can be made for any shape of headboard. The instructions include padding – even if your headboard is already padded, a padded cover gives a smooth, firm shape. The piped edge is optional, but it gives a neat, professional finish.

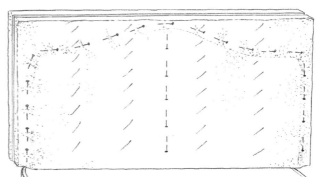

FABRIC AMOUNTS

Measure the width and depth of the headboard and add 10cm (4in) for seams and ease. For a single and double headboard cover, buy twice the depth. For queen and king sizes, buy three times the depth. For the amount of piping needed, measure up one side, across the top and down remaining side and add 10cm (4in) for seams.

YOU WILL NEED

(see page 52 for amounts)

❖ HEADBOARD of your choice
❖ FURNISHING FABRIC
❖ Mediumweight WADDING
❖ LINING FABRIC
❖ NEWSPAPER and PEN
❖ PINS and TAPE
❖ 40cm (½yd) contrast FABRIC 140cm (54in) wide for ties
❖ PIPING

▶ See pages 11-12 for piping details.

1 Cutting fabric From furnishing fabric, cut two rectangles to the measurements in Fabric Amounts, above. For queen or king size bed join panels to make the correct width – start with one fabric width and add panels to each side.

2 Join wadding Join wadding widths together to form two rectangles same size as fabric rectangles. Butt widths together and stitch across join with diagonal tacking which will not be removed. Position a wadding rectangle to wrong side of each fabric rectangle and tack layers together.

3 Shaping fabric Fold front panel in half widthways and pin along fold. Repeat with back. Use a tape measure and chalk or pins to mark the centre of headboard. Wrong sides together, pin front and back panels together at the centre and drop them over the headboard. Matching centre of fabric to centre headboard, continue to pin front and back together following outline of headboard. Remove cover and trim seam to 2cm (¾in) of pinned edge. Remove pins. Use front as pattern to cut two lining pieces.

4 Stitching ties Cut out and make up ties as given in steps 1 and 3 of Rectangular Tie-on Cover on the previous pages.

5 Adding piping Tack piping to right side of front cover, so seam of piping aligns with cover seamline, 2cm (¾in) in from outer edge. Snip into piping seam allowance at the corners to help ease it round.

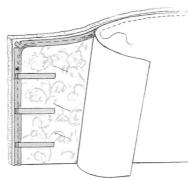

6 Joining front and back Pin then tack ties in place as in step 5 of Rectangular Tie-on Cover. Stitch ties in place. With right sides together, position back cover over front cover, and stitch around top edge, stopping 4cm (1½in) above each top tie. Clip across corners and trim wadding from seam. Turn to right side.

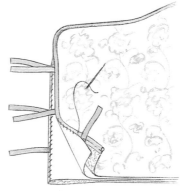

◀ *Contrast piping emphasizes how neatly this lightly padded cover fits over the shaped headboard.*

7 Adding lining Stitch lining panels together across top and down sides to top of ties. Press in side seam allowances. Push lining inside cover, with wrong sides together, and slipstitch side seams. Turn up lining and cover hems and machine or slipstitch together.

INSTANT SWAGS AND TAILS

A length of fabric, some masking tape, fabric adhesive or tacks, the most basic of poles and half an hour of time well spent are all that's required to recreate these sensational instant swag effects.

A swag with or without tails works alone as the only window dressing, or it may be paired with a blind or curtains for greater privacy and insulation. Gauzy sheers or soft printed cottons are ideal for making instant swag and tail effects.

Using lightweight fabrics means that the entire width of the fabric is required, eliminating the need for hemming the long edges and keeping sewing to a welcome minimum. The drapes are held in graceful folds by tacks or sticky tape, placed discreetly out of sight on the back of a curtain holdback, a thin pole or a length of lightweight dowelling.

Some styles are created using the latest gadgets such as metal valance creators which eliminate the need for a pole or any other fittings. The fabric is simply slipped through rings, mounted on each side of the window, and twisted into decorative rosettes or bows. A natural swag frames the top of the window while the ends of the fabric cascade down on either side to form short to floor-length tails. New fittings for creating instant curtain effects are constantly arriving on the market, so it's well worth investigating what's on offer.

Commercial swagholders are available from many soft furnishing stores. They are twists of metal, mounted to the wall on either side of the window. The fabric is pulled through the holders and twisted into mock rosettes. When measuring up the fabric remember to allow extra for each fabric twist.

ONE-PIECE SWAG AND TAILS

Use this heading on its own, with a blind or above a curtain as shown. Hang the curtain or blind first, using a plain plastic track, as it will be hidden by the drapery of the swag. The swag itself is draped over a pole, mounted slightly out from the wall. A wooden pole is fine, or use a length of dowel mounted on hooks. The swag is held in place with tacks or staples.

YOU WILL NEED

❖ CURTAIN POLE AND BRACKETS OR DOWEL AND HOOKS

❖ TAPE MEASURE

❖ FABRIC

❖ MASKING TAPE

❖ UPHOLSTERERS' TACKS OR STAPLE GUN

▶ *Sheer fabric, used copiously, provides privacy without sacrificing the view. The swag is formed by draping a length of the fabric over a separate pole.*

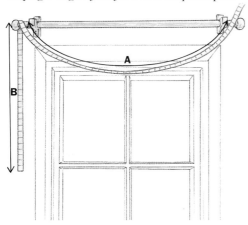

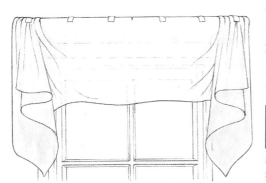

1 Measuring up For the swag, drape a tape measure between each end of the pole and note measurement (**A**). Measure down the side of the window to the desired length of one tail (**B**) and double the amount. Add these measurements together. To allow for fixing, add a further 30-40cm (12-16in) for the total amount of fabric required.

2 Preparing fabric Fold fabric in half widthways and mark centre. Mark centre of pole and, matching marks, tape one selvedge of fabric to back of pole.

3 Draping fabric Pick up each end of fabric and loop it back over the ends of the pole, holding it temporarily in place with pins or tape. Check the length of the tails and trim as required. Take down fabric and stitch double 1cm (⅜in) hems on each short end to neaten.

▼▼▼ TIP ▼▼▼

PRACTISE FIRST

It's a good idea to practise arranging the swag and tails effect before fixing it up at the window. Supporting the pole across two chair backs, drape the fabric over it, holding the folds in place with masking tape.

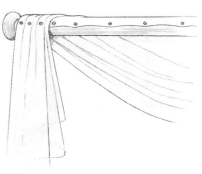

4 Securing fabric Rearrange the fabric on the pole, holding it temporarily in place with masking tape. Once you are satisfied with the result secure the fabric with tacks or staples at the back of the pole.

DOUBLE DRAPE

A fabric with a directional pattern can pose some problems with instant swag effects, if you want the pattern to hang in the same direction on each tail. The solution is to cut the tails and swag separately, then join the lengths back together again, reversing the direction of the print.

This treatment works for a narrow window where the swag is cut from just one fabric width. For a wider window, you need to cut and join widths to make the swag.

YOU WILL NEED

❖ Two Holdbacks

❖ Tape Measure

❖ Fabric

❖ Upholsterers' Tacks

1 Cutting swag Mount the holdbacks on the wall 10cm (4in) above the top corners of the window frame. Drape a tape measure between the holdbacks and measure the length of the swag. Add 20cm (8in) for seams and fixing. Cut a rectangle of fabric, across the fabric width, to this length by 60cm (23½in) deep. If necessary, join widths with 1.5cm (⅝in) flat seams to make up the desired width.

2 Cutting tails Measure from holdback to floor, double the measurement and add 20cm (8in) for hems. Cut fabric to this length. Cut each piece in half widthways then lengthways to give four lengths. For each tail, join two pieces along the short edges with right sides together so the print runs in opposite directions. Neaten seams.

3 Hemming Machine stitch a double 1cm (⅜in) hem on the long edges of the swag and tails. To check length, hang a tail over a holdback and pin up hem. Remove tail and hand or machine stitch hem, turning under the raw edge for 1cm (⅜in). Repeat for other tail.

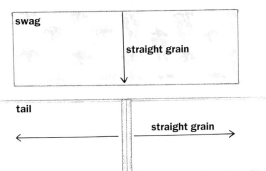

4 Draping fabrics Drape a tail over each holdback and temporarily secure with tape. Hang the swag from each holdback, tucking the raw edges under the tails.

5 Adjusting swag Arrange the folds of the swag until pleased with the effect. Then secure with a few tacks, inserted into the back or stem of holdback so that they are hidden by drapery.

◀ *The dainty floral swag, used to frame this window, is itself a focal point in the room. The swag is made by draping the fabric over metal holdbacks.*

RUCHED SWAG

This swag is gathered up by two casings and hung in place from two small hooks. The curtain underneath can be mounted on a pole, track or plastic-covered wire.

YOU WILL NEED

❖ TAPE MEASURE

❖ FABRIC

❖ TWO CUP HOOKS

❖ COTTON (TWILL) TAPE 12mm (½in) wide

1 **Preparing the fabric** Mount two cup hooks slightly above either side of the window frame. Drape a tape measure over the hooks, to work out the length of fabric required for making the tails and swag. Cut a length of fabric to this measurement. Turn up and stitch a double 1cm (³⁄₈in) hem on the short edges of fabric.

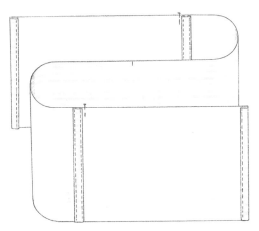

2 **Making the casings** Cut two 3cm (1¼in) wide strips across the fabric width. Press under 6mm (¼in) on the raw edges of each strip. Measure the distance between the cup hooks and mark this measurement centrally on the length of fabric. With wrong sides facing, tack strips across fabric width at each mark. Topstitch close to edges of each strip.

◤ *A simple swag, made to match the generous drapes, is the perfect choice for this child's room. The lightweight fabric provides privacy, yet still allows light to filter into the room.*

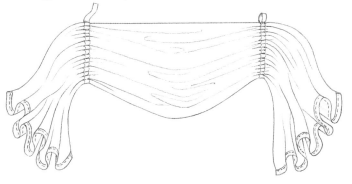

The delicate drapes of this window treatment, hung without any track at all, are designed to be opened and closed by tiebacks. The drapes are tacked in place to the window frame. The swag is formed by one strip of fabric, draped then tacked in place on either side of the frame. The tacks and raw ends of the swag are hidden by two choux rosettes.

3 **Putting up the swag** Thread tape through each casing. Secure one end of tape to casing with a few firm handstitches, then pull up tape to gather swag. Trim ends of tape, leaving enough to stitch the end into a small loop. Hang each loop over a cup hook.

TAB HEADED CURTAINS

Tab headed curtains are quick, easy and economical to make and lend themselves to formal and informal styles of decor. This version, made with contrast borders and tabs, has immediate impact.

Tab headed curtains are suspended from a pole by loops of fabric set at regular intervals along the top edge. They are not as expensive to make as conventional curtains with gathered headings because they use far less fabric, but they will still cover the window fully when drawn.

The tabs can be made in the same or a contrasting fabric, and can be any width. Ensure there are enough tabs to

support the curtain – a space of two tab widths between each tab is suggested – and match the width of the tab to the weight of the fabric and the pole size.

Whether looped on to a thick wood pole with carved finials or hung from a slim wrought iron one, tab headed curtains look great in a variety of different rooms. This lined version features a border and tabs made from a contrasting fabric of similar weight.

Curtains with a tab heading look handsome in all sorts of room settings – a tab heading is an economical choice, too, as it uses less fabric than conventional gathered headings.

MAKING A BORDERED TAB HEADING

Tab headed curtains hang slightly below the pole, so make sure your pole is at least 5cm (2in) above the top of the window, or light and draughts will come through the gap between the pole and top of the curtain. To calculate the length of the actual curtain, measure from a point 5cm (2in) below the base of the pole to the floor or just below the window as preferred. The width depends on how full you want the curtains to look when drawn. For curtains which lie flat against the window, you will only need fabric the width of the window, plus extra for seams. For a fuller effect, add half or a whole fabric width to each curtain. These curtains are made with a 5cm (2in) border and tabs. Seams of 1.5cm (⅝in) are included throughout.

▶ *Bordered tab headed curtains also make splendid bed drapes, with their loops threaded over the metal frame of a four poster.*

YOU WILL NEED

- ❖ CURTAIN FABRIC
- ❖ CONTRAST BORDER FABRIC
- ❖ IRON-ON INTERFACING for borders and tabs.
- ❖ LINING FABRIC
- ❖ SEWING THREAD
- ❖ TAPE MEASURE

1 Cutting curtains and lining Work out the curtain width and length. To allow for border subtract 3.5cm (1⅜in) from outer edge – this leaves 1.5cm (⅝in) for seams. Cut out the main fabric and lining to this size, joining widths where necessary.

2 Cutting borders Cut two side borders of contrast fabric 13cm (5¼in) wide by curtain length. Cut a hem border 13cm (5¼in) wide by curtain width plus 13cm (5¼in). Cut two heading borders 8cm (3¼in) wide by curtain width plus 13cm (5¼in). Cut interfacing to match. Fuse to wrong side.

3 Cutting tabs Each finished tab should be same width as border – 5cm (2in). Measure curtain top for number of tabs. Allow a space of two tab widths between each. Cut a 23 x 13cm (9 x 5in) strip from contrast fabric and interlining for each. For thick poles cut tabs longer, testing length.

4 Making the tabs Fuse interfacing to wrong side of each tab. With right sides together, fold each tab in half lengthways and stitch long edge. Turn tabs right side out, centre seam with allowances open, then press.

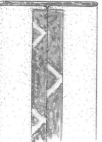

5 Joining side borders and lining With wrong sides together, press side borders in half lengthwise. Position a border to each edge of right side curtain, matching raw edges. Tack in place. Position lining, right sides together, to curtain. Stitch outer edges. Turn curtain to right side and press.

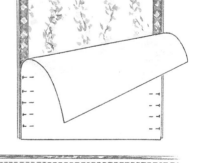

6 Adding hem border Right sides together, stitch hem border to lower edge of curtain/lining sandwich. Press seams to border, then press under 1.5cm (⅝in) hem on remaining raw edge and each short end. Right sides together, press border in half and stitch across short ends taking care not to catch main fabric. Clip corners and turn border to right side. Hand or machine stitch loose edge down.

7 Adding heading border and tabs Right sides together, position one border to top edge of curtain and stitch taking a 1.5cm (⅝in) seam. Press seams to border. Fold each tab in half with seam to inside and, matching raw edges, position to top edge of heading border. Space evenly and stitch.

8 Adding border facing Press under 1.5cm (⅝in) hem on one long raw edge of remaining border. Position it, right sides together and matching raw edges, over tabs. Stitch short ends and across top. Clip across corners and turn to right side. Machine or hand stitch raw edge down.

CURTAIN TIEBACKS

A pretty and practical way to dress up a window, tiebacks are easy and inexpensive to make and can give a new lease of life to dull, old curtains as well as adding the finishing touch to new ones.

By catching the curtains back at just the right height, tiebacks pull the fabric into an attractive sweep and allow more natural light into the room. Wide, full curtains drape into deep scoops of fabric, while narrow drapes can be elegantly tied back against the frame.

To make tiebacks you need only a remnant of fabric which blends or contrasts with the curtains. When you are making tiebacks for existing curtains but don't have any of the original fabric, choose another similar one.

Tiebacks can be made in a variety of shapes and styles, with different trims to suit your taste. You can make plain straight tiebacks, but they work more effectively and look better if shaped to give a tailored finish. As a trim add contrasting piping all round or stitch a frill along the lower edge.

CHOOSING FABRICS

Most medium or lightweight closely woven furnishing fabrics are suitable. Heavy brocades or velvet are best avoided as they are too bulky.

Use furnishing fabric for both sides of the tieback unless you are short of fabric, or it's bulky or very expensive, in which case use a lining fabric for the back piece.

A simple shaped tieback with top stitching holds this curtain back in a shallow swag.

POSITIONING TIEBACKS

To work out where to place the tiebacks and how long and wide they should be, loop a tape measure around the curtain at several heights until you find the appropriate place. Adjust the curtain to create the folds and draped effect you want, then make a note of the length of the loop. With the tape measure still looped around the curtains, make a pencil mark on the wall or window surround behind the draped fabric for the hook, checking that the outer curtain edge will hang straight.

On sill length curtains the tiebacks are usually positioned about two-thirds of the way down, but on longer and floor length curtains there's scope for choosing various positions. Each position affects the look of a window, so choose carefully to suit its shape.

In general, the lower the tiebacks the fuller the drape of the curtains but the more the view and natural light are obscured. This can be an advantage if the view isn't special. If the view is good and the window small, extend the curtain track on to the wall at either side of the window, draw the curtains back and use tiebacks to hold the fabric off the window in decorative drapes.

Tiebacks for sill length curtains
Tiebacks placed about two-thirds of the way down sill length curtains will part them in gentle folds on either side to frame the window and let in plenty of light.

Sill height tiebacks
On floor length curtains at a small window, with the tiebacks arranged at sill height, the fabric is swept into generous curves above the tiebacks and drapes well below.

Placed high
Positioned one-third of the way down from the top of the curtain, the tiebacks let in more light and give the impression the window is of greater length.

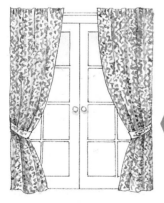

Placed low
Tiebacks set two-thirds of the way down the curtain create a full effect at the top which makes a narrow window seem wider but may cut out a lot of natural light.

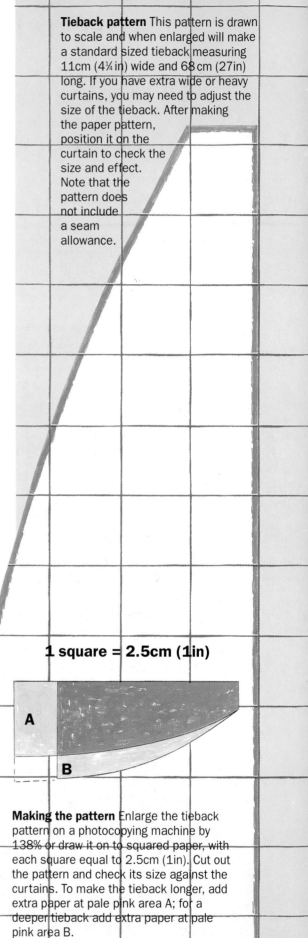

Tieback pattern This pattern is drawn to scale and when enlarged will make a standard sized tieback measuring 11cm (4¼in) wide and 68cm (27in) long. If you have extra wide or heavy curtains, you may need to adjust the size of the tieback. After making the paper pattern, position it on the curtain to check the size and effect. Note that the pattern does not include a seam allowance.

1 square = 2.5cm (1in)

A

B

Making the pattern Enlarge the tieback pattern on a photocopying machine by 138% or draw it on to squared paper, with each square equal to 2.5cm (1in). Cut out the pattern and check its size against the curtains. To make the tieback longer, add extra paper at pale pink area A; for a deeper tieback add extra paper at pale pink area B.

FOLD LINE

SIMPLE SHAPED TIEBACKS

1 Cutting out
Positioning pattern so any design will be well displayed at front of tiebacks, cut out on the fold two pieces of fabric (or one piece fabric, one lining), adding 1.5cm (⅝in) seam allowance all round. For each tieback cut out one interfacing on the fold without seam allowance.

2 Adding the interfacing
Lay the interfacing centrally on the wrong side of the front piece of fabric and iron in place. Fold the seam allowance over the interfacing and pin then tack in place, pleating or snipping into the allowance as necessary so it lies flat.

3 Attaching the back piece
Turn under and press a 2cm (¾in) hem to the wrong side all round the back piece. Centre and pin it over the tieback interfacing with wrong sides together. Neatly hand stitch the back and front together all round the edge; remove pins and tacking stitches.

4 Finishing off If you wish, machine topstitch along the lower edge using matching thread. Hand stitch the rings to the centre of both ends on each tieback. To position the hooks, loop the tieback round the curtain at several heights before marking their place on the wall or window frame. Fix the hooks, making sure they are level.

FRILLED TIEBACKS

These can be quickly made using a sewing machine to attach the frill. The materials are the same as for the shaped tiebacks, but allow extra fabric for the frill.

1 Cutting out Follow steps 1 and 2 of Shaped Tiebacks but leave the seam allowance on the lower edge free. For a frill 6cm (2¼in) deep, cut out a fabric strip 1½ times the length of the tieback by 15cm (6in) wide.

2 Making the frill Fold the frill in half lengthways with right sides together; pin and then stitch seams at each end. Trim, turn right side out and press. Through both layers run a line of gathering threads 1 and 2cm (⅜ and ¾in) from the raw edge along the length of the frill.

3 Attaching the frill Pull up the gathering threads so that the frill is the same length as the lower edge of the tieback, and tack it to the right side of the front piece, matching raw edges. With right sides together, place the back piece on top. Tack and machine stitch the lower edge together using the interfacing edge as the seam line.

4 Finishing off Turn the tieback right side out, press thoroughly then turn in a 2cm (¾in) seam allowance round the top and side edges on the back piece. Pin then hand stitch in place to the front piece. Finally add the rings and hooks.

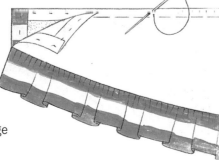

PIPED TIEBACKS

Adding piping around the edge of a tieback emphasizes its shape against the curtain as well as possibly introducing an accent colour. In addition to the materials for the shaped tiebacks, you need two lengths of covered piping to trim the outer edges. (See pages 11-12 for full details on how to make piping.)

1 Cutting out Follow step 1 of Shaped Tiebacks for cutting out the interfacing and fabric. Then iron the interfacing in place as before.

2 Adding the piping Make enough covered piping to fit all round the tiebacks. Tack the piping around the right side of the interfaced piece of fabric using the interfacing edge as a stitch line. Clip into the corners. Take care to position the piping join where it will be hidden behind the curtain. Machine stitch in place using a zipper foot.

3 Adding the backing Press the seam allowances to the wrong side and tack in place. Turn under and press 1.5cm (⅝ in) seam allowance all round the tieback back piece. Pin to the front piece with wrong sides together and hand stitch in place. Finish by sewing the rings to the tiebacks and fix hooks.

TIP

TIEBACK TEAM
To help coordinate new tiebacks which are in a different fabric from the existing curtains, buy extra fabric and make or trim a pelmet (valance) above the window, or cover cushions on nearby chair.

GOBLET PLEATED CURTAINS

The chic, structured nature of goblet pleats, and the ample folds they form, make them ideal for traditional, full length window dressings.

G oblet pleats are one of the most elegant of curtain headings. The cylindrical shape of each pleat holds drapes of fabric in deep, rounded folds that draw back into scoops of cloth, but which hang beautifully in gentle columns. To complement this style choose mediumweight fabrics that drape well and are neither too fine nor too bulky to hold the shape of the pleats.

The striking feature of the curtains is the sculptured shape of each goblet. To accent the effect, stitch a border trim along the upper edge and to emphasize the neck of each goblet, stitch a rosette, fabric covered button

or braid detail in a line across the curtain, giving a completely individual look to your window dressing. A pole or track fixture is suitable for goblet pleating as the eye is drawn to the top of the curtain and it is a good opportunity to make the most of an interesting curtain rod and finials.

Goblet pleats are easy to make. All you need is a purpose-made heading tape stitched along the top of a simple lined curtain panel. Despite their lavish appearance, the goblet heading tape gathering allowance is only twice the window width so they are not an overly expensive type of curtain heading.

Sunny yellow goblet pleated curtains hang from a wrought iron rail which has fleur-de-lys style finials. A double row of golden cord loops under each goblet emphasizes the gracious shape of the design.

GOBLET HEADING TAPE

These instructions show you how to apply goblet heading tape to a basic lined curtain. If the curtains hang in front or below the curtain fixture, measure the curtain length from the top or bottom of the fixture respectively. When placing the tape along the width of the curtain, decide whether you want the usual overlap of flat fabric at the ends and in the middle and position the heading tape pleats accordingly. To ensure a pronounced finish to each goblet a few handstitches at the top and bottom holds each pleat neatly.

YOU WILL NEED

❖ FURNISHING FABRIC
❖ LINING FABRIC
❖ CONTRASTING FABRIC FOR TOP EDGE (optional)
❖ TAPE MEASURE
❖ MATCHING THREAD
❖ GOBLET HEADING TAPE
❖ TISSUE PAPER OR CARDBOARD TUBE
❖ CURTAIN HOOKS
❖ TRIMMINGS (optional)

1 Measuring for curtains Fit the curtain pole or track in position at the window. Measure from the fixture to the floor or desired height. Add 14cm (5½in) for the heading and hem. For the total width, allow twice the width of the curtain fixture plus 4cm (1½in) for side hems and 3cm (1¼in) for joining widths.

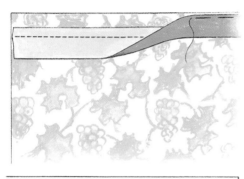

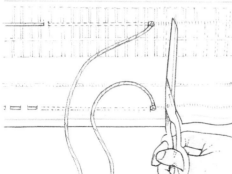

6 Positioning heading tape Position tape so goblet pleats at either end are the same distance from curtain edge, with the distance between the first pleat and edge of curtains no greater than the distance between the pleats. Pin tape on the right side of the fabric, overlapping the top edge of the curtain by 1cm (⅜in). Machine stitch the tape in place along the top sewing line.

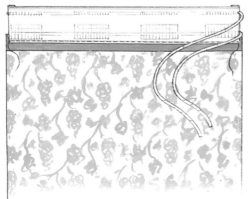

2 Cutting out Cut the curtain fabric to the measurements given in step 1. Join the fabric widths with plain flat seams if required, and press the seams open. Cut out and stitch the lining to make a panel 5cm (2in) narrower and 15cm (6in) shorter than the curtain.

3 Adding top edge trim (optional) Cut a strip of contrast fabric 5.5cm (2⅛in) deep by the width of the curtain fabric. Right sides together, position strip 2.5cm (1½in) down from top edge. Stitch a 1.5cm (⅝in) seam. Press seam and strip to right side. Pin then tack strip and top edge of curtain together. Treat curtain fabric and border as one.

5 Trimming tape cords With tape right way up – so goblet stems pinch at the bottom of the tape – pull out the top cord of the first full pleat, on the right end. Measure 4.5cm (1¾in) in from this point and pull out and knot top and bottom cords at this position. Trim tape and cords 1cm (⅜in) from the knots and turn under 2.5cm (1in) of the tape so knotted ends are turned under.

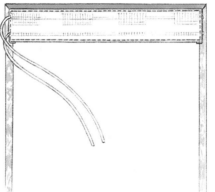

7 Sewing heading tape Fold over the heading tape and 1.5cm (⅝in) of the top edge of the curtain to the back, neatening corners. At the left end, pull the cords free and turn under 2.5cm (1in) in line with the curtain edge. Machine stitch the heading tape along the bottom sewing line and across either end.

4 Lining curtains Mark centre of the top and lower edge on both fabric and lining. Right sides together, pin and stitch sides stopping 18cm (7½in) from lower curtain edges. Turn to right side, so centre marks match and there is a 2.5cm (1in) fabric border either side of lining. Press.

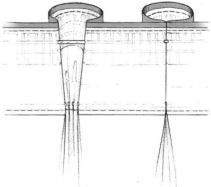

8 Pulling up pleats Pull the top cord of the tape first, position the pleat and then pull the bottom cord to form pinch pleats at the stem of the goblet. Advance position of this pleat to form the second pleat and start to remake a pleat at the position of the first. Advance the pleats until you have covered the width of the curtain with the pleats.

TIP

SEWING HEADING TAPE
To make sure the tape is not
distorted when you sew it, stitch
the top and bottom edges in
the same direction.

9 Neatening pleats Make a few
stitches in the heading tape at
top and bottom of each goblet.
Then make small securing stitches on
the front of curtain at the bottom of
pleat. Pad out goblets with crumpled
tissue or cardboard tube. Insert hooks
in pockets at back of each pleat.

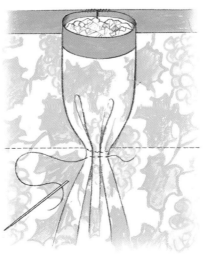

▲ *Mellow honey colours bring a warm
glow to a long bedroom window
dressed with goblet pleated curtains.
A narrow band of fabric skimming the
upper edge of the curtains emphasizes
the sculptured shape of each pleat.*

10 Hemming the curtains Turn up and
press a 5cm (2in) then a 7.5cm (3in)
hem on the curtains. Hand stitch the
hem, mitring corners. Turn up, press and
machine stitch a 2.5cm (1in) double hem
on the lining. Slip stitch down the loose
side edges of the lining.

DECORATIVE TRIMMINGS

To emphasize the sculptured shape and elegant lines of goblet headed curtains, be creative and add a fabric border or a small, well-chosen decorative trim to the base of each goblet pleat.

▶ *A pattern of strong stripes follows the line of curtain drapes from a button detail, sewn at the stem of each plump pleat. Wooden holdbacks repeat the roundness of the buttons and suit the simplicity of the window treatment.*

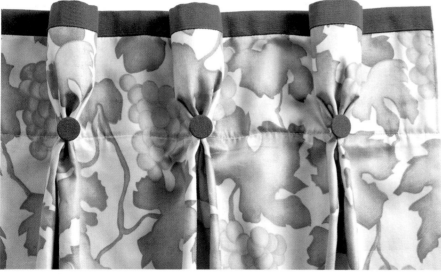

◀ *Goblet pleated curtains are a good choice for a formal living room. The fabric choice, showing an elegant grape and leaf pattern, reinforces the formality of the goblet heading.*

▶ *A Flemish knotted cord trim is a traditional way of finishing a goblet heading. The cord is hand-stitched in place at the base of each goblet.*

Heading tapes

A well chosen heading tape adds a final flourish to your curtains.

Ready-made heading tapes are much the easiest way of gathering the top of a curtain or valance. The tapes are available in a range of different styles and depths, and are attached by being stitched flat to the top of the curtain or valance. They have cords threaded through them, so that when the cords are pulled up, neat gathers or pleats (depending on the style of the tape) are formed.

For a complete glossary of curtain styles, see pages 81-84.

For a complete glossary of curtain styles, see pages 81-84.

TIP

ADJUSTING WIDTHS
The final width of your curtains can be varied greatly by making the pleats or gathers more or less tight. However, with triple and cylindrical pleats there is less flexibility for altering the width of the curtain.

What heading tape?

The choice of heading tape depends on your own preference and the style of curtain required. **Traditional style** heading tapes which are readily available include gathered; pencil pleated; box pleated; triple pleated and cylindrical. Of these gathered, pencil pleated and triple pleated are sold in a choice of three different depths. There are also special tapes for sheer and net curtains. These are made in lightweight, almost translucent material. Three **novelty styles,** vogue, smocked and Tudor ruff, are also quite widely sold.

As a general guideline, relate the depth of the tape to the length of the curtain – deep heading tapes (triple pleated and cylindrical) are best suited to long formal curtains. Tapes sold in narrow depths (gathered or pencil pleated) work for shorter or sill length curtains.

Heading tapes have pockets or loops designed to take the curtain hooks. Each style of tape requires its own specific hook – check the manufacturer's instructions.

The type of hook will also depend on how you want to hang the curtain – with most tapes the hooks can be positioned in different levels on the tape to allow the curtain to be hung either from a pole or up over a curtain track. However, some of the triple pleated tapes can be hung in only one way – always check the manufacturer's instructions on the packet carefully before buying.

What fabric?

All the tapes are suitable for most fabrics although, again, try and marry the tape to the fabric – for instance a simple gathered heading would be best with a light unlined cotton curtain, while a triple or cylindrical pleat would suit heavy velvet. Plain fabrics benefit from a very decorative heading tape, while a print may require only a simple style.

Check the weight and drapability of the fabric too: a heavy fabric does not gather up well into pencil pleats but suits the drama of cylindrical pleats. A fabric that hangs well – such as a mediumweight shantung – suits triple pleats, which release the fabric into deep folds, while a very light flimsy fabric, such as voile, is best gathered.

Tapes can be laundered or drycleaned, so follow the care instructions for the curtain fabric when laundering the finished curtains.

Tape and fabric amounts

The different headings require different amounts of fabric. As a guide: gathered headings need 1½ times the track width of fabric; box and pencil pleats take 2½ times the track width; triple and cylindrical pleats need 3 times. For sheer or net curtains allow at least 2 times the track width.

You will need the same amount of tape as the total flat width of all the curtains, plus extra for finishing the tape ends and placing pleats – allow about 34cm (⅜yd) extra per curtain.

For more information on calculating fabric amounts see pages 79-80.

For more information on calculating fabric amounts see pages 79-80.

Linings

There are tapes available for making detachable linings. These gather up the lining heading separately. The curtain hooks catch both the lining and the main fabric to the pole or track.

For curtains which have attached linings, make up the curtain with its lining first, then add the heading tape of your choice.

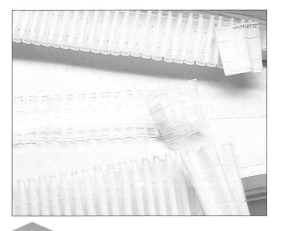

➤ *A vogue heading tape, one of several novelty styles, gathers the curtain fabric into a very elegant effect. A deep tape such as this is best suited to long, formal curtains.*

Gripping tapes

The newest style of heading tape works without a track or pole – it simply sticks to an adhesive strip that is pressed on to a wall. It is ideal for curtains that do not need to be drawn, windows that are an awkward shape or pelmets (valances). The actual heading tape is stitched to the curtain top in the usual way.

Traditional style tapes

Gathered pleat

This tape is suitable for all fabrics and produces a simple, attractive heading that's ideal for informal or country style curtains. *You need fabric 1½ times the curtain track width.*

Pencil pleat

Suitable for most settings, this heading tape gives a neat, elegant look to curtains. It comes in different depths to match the curtain lengths and weights – deeper headings will give a better proportion on longer curtains. *You need fabric 2½ times the track width.*

Box pleat

A formal heading tape, box pleats emphasize the curtain length. The pleats show up well on plain fabrics; they are also ideal for valances on chairs, settees and dressing tables. *You need fabric 2½ times the track width.*

Cylindrical pleat

This is a good choice for curtains in heavier fabrics or interlined curtains. Take care to match the pleats across the centre opening unless curtains overlap. *You need fabric 3 times the track width.*

Sheers

There are a couple of heading tapes suitable for very lightweight lace or sheer curtains. The tapes are made in a light mesh material – the one shown here gathers the curtain up into pencil pleats. *You need fabric 2 times the track width.*

Triple pleat

This heading tape makes the curtain drape well and it is available in three different depths. It is best for mediumweight fabrics. Position the tape so that the pleats fall evenly across the curtains with equal space at each end. *You need fabric 3 times the track width.*

Novelty style tapes

Tudor ruff

This type of heading is a decorative alternative to the pencil pleat and is ideal for jazzing up plain fabrics. *You need fabric 2 times the track width.*

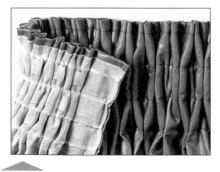

Smocked

This effect was once the craft of the professional curtain maker. It is extremely decorative and looks good on both plain and patterned fabrics. It is particularly popular on nets and sheers. *You need fabric 2 times the track width.*

Vogue

Similar to a Tudor ruff heading, this tape gives a stylish and elegant effect. *You need fabric 2 times the track width.*

SIMPLE SHEER CURTAINS

Today's sheer curtains are light, filmy lengths of patterned or plain fabric that let sunlight filter into a room creating an airy feel.

Stylish new fabrics, woven or printed with exquisite designs and trimmed with delicate borders, bring fresh style to sheer curtains. These new printed sheers perform the traditional role of screening out direct sunlight, while their patterns and prints cast a light breezy aura across the room.

When choosing your fabric bear in mind the room's use. What looks marvellous in a bathroom may not have the sophistication needed for the more formal setting of a living or dining area. Coordinating sheer and standard furnishing fabrics are also widely available, making mix and match schemes easy to achieve.

If there is an unattractive outlook from a window, opt for lightweight, opaque curtains. They hide the view and provide privacy, while still allowing any daylight to bathe the room.

Translucent heading tapes, designed specifically for sheer curtains, are available in a range of pleat styles. They are balanced and sized to suit lightweight fabrics, forming fine folds and drapes. For fixed curtains (those that do not need to be drawn) there are also heading tapes with an in-built touch and close fastening strip, eliminating the need for a track and hooks. The strip is attached to the window frame or surround, and the completed curtains are pressed in place.

A delicate blue floral pattern reinforces the fragile appeal of these sheer drapes. The pencil pleat heading provides sufficient fullness to ensure the curtains look generous, while the wrought iron pole provides a rugged foil to their prettiness.

71

MAKING THE CURTAINS

Making sheer curtains is very similar to making simple unlined curtains, except that the seams are self-neatening and hems have to be double to disguise raw edges. These instructions include methods for neatening both side and base hems. If you have chosen a fabric of the correct width, with trimmed or neatened selvedge edges, just stitch the lower hems and add a heading tape.

Alternatively, if you have chosen a sheer to a specified length with a decorative trimmed or neatened lower edge, and a ready-made heading, you only need to stitch the side edges.

If you are adding a heading tape, you must provide a firm foundation with a double hem, the width of the tape, all along the upper edge.

Sheer fabrics are slippery, which makes them hard to cut. To make it easier, cover the cutting surface with an old sheet, then lay the sheer on top and cut one layer at a time. A metre stick helps in measuring up and straightening the raw end, as its weight stops the fabric from moving.

▶ See pages 79-80 for measuring up and hemming curtains and pages 73-74 for stitching sheer fabrics.

1 Calculating fabric amounts Measure the window width, add 8cm (3¼in) for both side hems and, if joining widths, an extra 3cm (1¼in) for every seam. Multiply this width of fabric according to gathering allowance for heading tape chosen. Measure the window height, adding 8cm (3¼in) for the base hem plus twice the width of the heading tape.

3 Stitching the hems Turn under a 2cm (¾in) double hem along both side edges. Pin, tack and machine stitch both side hems. Turn under a 4cm (1½in) double hem along the base edge, forming neat corners. Pin and stitch base hem.

4 Neatening the top edge Turn under and press the top edge of the curtain to make a double hem just less than the width of the heading tape. Position the tape along the top edge and pin in place.

5 Stitching on heading tape Tack and machine stitch the heading tape in place, trimming and turning in the raw ends for 1cm (⅜in). Leave the gathering cords loose at one end and catch them down at opposite end.

2 Cutting out Lay the fabric flat and trim the base edge straight. Measure the curtain length up from base edge and, using chalk, mark the top edge. Cut across the fabric following the marked line. Repeat, as necessary. Stitch widths together with flat fell seams.

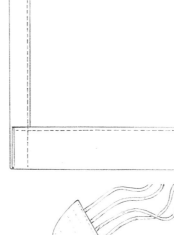

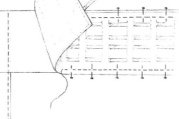

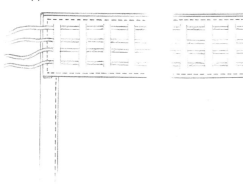

6 Pleating up curtains Pull up the heading tapes tightly to set the pleats in position, then gently ease out until the curtain is the correct width for the window. Insert the curtain hooks, placing one at each end and the rest spaced approximately 8cm (3¼in) apart.

◥ *With a double layer of sheer curtains, you can sweep back the top set, leaving the lower ones permanently drawn to maintain privacy. A smocked heading provides a crisp finish.*

TIP

SHRINK PROOF
Sheer fabrics, especially in cotton, may shrink. As a preventative measure, you can either pre-shrink this type of fabric by washing it before sewing or, if you prefer, stitch a triple, rather than a double hem. Then if the curtains shrink there is an allowance to let down.

Sewing sheer fabrics

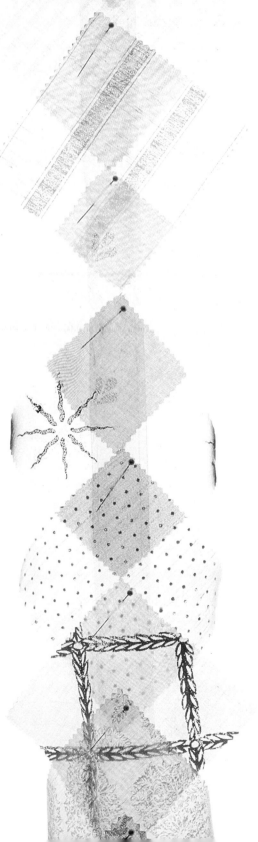

Well sewn sheer fabrics bring a delicate beauty to any room.

Sheer fabrics play an important part in the home – from net curtains which provide privacy, to filmy voiles swathing windows or creating enchanting bed drapes. The most popular sheers used for soft furnishings are crisp voiles, organza and nets or softer muslin, fine cottons and linens.

The most important point to remember when working with sheer fabrics is that the stitches, seams and hems will show through to the right side, so they must be as fine and unobtrusive as possible.

To minimize the sewing involved in making sheer curtains you can buy sheer curtain fabric with ready finished edges. Lengths with decorative, shaped base edges and ready made slot headings are available in a variety of drops from 90-228cm (36-90in). You can also get hold of café curtains with shorter drops, from 30cm (12in), with slot headings or holes woven along the top edge for threading on to a café rod.

A variety of widths is available with the convenience of ready finished sides. With these, you simply have to hem the curtain and add a heading tape or casing.

You can buy complete sheer curtains and panels as well, which require no sewing at all.

Working with sheers

To ensure success when sewing sheer fabrics it is important to handle the fabric carefully and use the correct equipment, as the delicate quality of the fabric means you can easily mark or snag it. Always use sharp pins and needles, for example, otherwise they can catch the fabric.

Materials and tools
Machine needles Use size 70 (9) or 80 (11).
Hand needles Use size 8, 9 or 10.
Pins Use super fine (lace) pins, 0.5mm diameter, to avoid making pinholes. Silk pins are too thick.
Sewing thread Stitch with extra fine threads in mercerized cotton, cotton/polyester or silk.
Interfacing Use sheer, non-woven fusible or sew-in interfacing, organza or self-fabric, which means using the main sheer fabric as the interfacing.

Scissors or **rotary cutter** Make sure you use sharp scissors to avoid snagging the fabric. Alternatively use a rotary cutter with a new blade – it does not move the fabric as you cut. Sharp pinking shears are useful for neatening raw edges but make sure the blades of the shears are well aligned.
Marker Use a pencil with a soft lead, tailors' chalk, fabric marker or a pen with disappearing, air-erasable ink. Draw gently across the fabric to avoid dragging the delicate threads.

Preparing the fabric
Certain sheers should be pre-shrunk before sewing. When buying the fabric, check the care instructions on the roll of fabric or ask the shop assistant. Allow an extra 30cm (12in) for shrinkage when needed.

On sheer curtains you can turn up a temporary hem and let it down to the correct length after washing. Washing also removes the stiff, starchy finish of some fabrics and makes stitching easier. If using an interfacing or lining make sure that this is pre-shrunk too, before sewing it to the sheer fabric.

TIP

WASHING SHEERS
Handwash sheers in warm water with a mild detergent – machine washing may damage open nets and voiles. Before quite dry, stretch the fabric to regain length and width. Iron slightly damp on a cool setting. Do not twist or wring the fabric. Do not dryclean.

Cutting sheer fabrics
Sheer fabrics are often quite slippery and tend to slide out of position when you are cutting them. To prevent this, cover the cutting area with another fabric such as an old sheet. Alternatively, cut them out on a well padded work surface or use a rotary cutter on a cardboard cutting mat. Pin the sheer fabric to the cutting surface, placing the pins in the seam allowance.

Stitching sheer fabrics

Always pin, then tack sheer fabrics before stitching them as they tend to move around as you sew, which distorts the position of the seams. Push the pins and tacks through the fabric of the seam allowance, concealing any marks within the seam.

To ensure smooth machine stitching, fit a new needle and adjust the settings on your sewing machine. Reduce the upper tension slightly and have the pressure regulator at a light setting. Fit an even-feed foot so that the fabric runs smoothly through the machine. Keep stitches small – 12-16 stitches per 2.5cm (1in). Run test stitches on a scrap of the fabric to check any adjustments you make. For practice stitching always sew through the same number of fabric layers as the actual stitching.

Seams

The best type of seams for sheer fabrics are narrow self-neatening seams, which fully enclose all the raw edges. Use Mock French seams or, for a quicker result, zigzaged or overlocked seams. *French* and *flat fell* seams are also ideal; instructions for these seams are given on pages 31-32.

Mock French seams

Place the two pieces of fabric together with right sides facing. Pin, tack and stitch a 1.5cm (⅝in) seam. Turn under seam allowances 6mm (¼in) into the seam and press. Match the folded edges, pin together and stitch close to the fold.

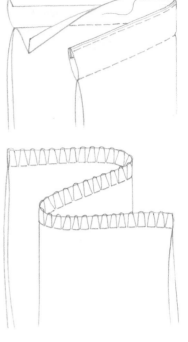

Zigzagged seam

Place the two pieces of fabric together with right sides facing. Pin, tack and stitch a 1.5cm (⅝in) seam. Working inside the seam allowance, stitch the seam again with a narrow zigzag stitch. Trim the seam allowance close to the zigzag stitches with sharp scissors.

Overlocked seam

An overlocker stitches, trims and neatens the fabric all at the same time. To use an overlocker place the two pieces of fabric together with right sides facing and stitch a 1.5cm (⅝in) seam.

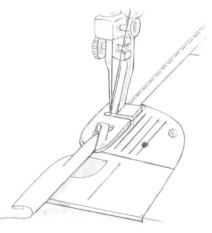

Hems

To maximize the draping quality of sheers, use a hem of less than 1cm (⅜in). Alternatively, use 4cm (½in) double hems.

Machine hem

Fit a hemming foot to the sewing machine. Trim the hem allowance to 6mm (¼in). Fold under a double 3mm (⅛in) hem and crease along the hem edge for 5cm (2in). Place the hem under the foot and stitch a few stitches through the creased fold. With the needle still in the fabric, raise the presser foot and guide the raw edge of the fabric through the scroll of the hemming foot. Lower the foot again and continue stitching, guiding fabric through the foot and holding fabric taut behind the foot.

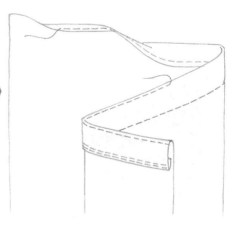

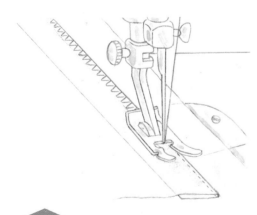

Hairline hem

Machine stitch along hemline and trim the hem to 6mm (¼in). Turn under the hem so stitching sits just inside hem and press. To prevent fabric slipping, place a strip of tissue paper under it. Working from the right side, through fabric and tissue paper, stitch along the folded edge with a short, narrow zigzag stitch. Tear away the paper and trim hem allowance close to the stitches.

Topstitched hem

Using sharp scissors, trim the hem allowance to 1.5cm (⅝in). Turn under 6mm (¼in) and, working from the wrong side of the fabric edge, stitch close to the fold. Turn under and press a further 1cm (⅜in) and edge stitch as close to both folds of the hem as possible.

TWO-PART CURTAINS

Curtains with detachable linings give you the best of both worlds.
Attach the lining in winter months for extra warmth, and remove it in the
summer for lighter, airier drapes, and also for cleaning.

Curtains with detachable linings are wonderfully versatile and very easy to make. First you need to make a simple, unlined curtain – this is just a rectangle of fabric, gathered with a heading tape along the top edge and hemmed along the remaining three edges. The detachable lining is made in exactly the same way as the curtain, but using a special pocketed lining heading tape.

The curtain and lining are held together by the curtain hooks, which pass through both the lining and the curtain heading tape; snap

Read all about cutting out curtains on pages 79-80.

fasteners stitched down the sides of the lining and curtain also hold the layers together. This makes the lining very easy to remove when you want to launder or dry clean the curtains – a useful option if the two fabrics have different care requirements.

In the summer months, you can use unlined curtains on their own to create a light, airy look around the window. They provide privacy while still filtering sunlight into the room. In colder months, you can attach the removable lining to provide instant insulation.

Lightweight, unlined curtains diffuse bright light to a restful glow. During winter months, you can add a detachable lining for extra warmth.

MAKING UNLINED CURTAINS

You can make unlined curtains with most styles of heading tape, and attach them to a curtain track or pole. As the backs of the curtains are on view through the window, use self-neatening seams such as French or flat fell seams. Take care to match up any design motifs across the fabric widths and leading edges. See page 80 for calculating fabric amounts.

See page 80 for calculating fabric amounts.

YOU WILL NEED

- ❖ CURTAIN FABRIC
- ❖ HEADING TAPE
- ❖ MATCHING SEWING THREAD
- ❖ CURTAIN HOOKS

1 Cutting out the fabric widths Measure up the window for curtains of the desired size. Allowing for fullness, seams, hems and matching patterns, cut out the required number of fabric widths.

2 Stitching widths together Taking care to match fabric motifs, tack the widths together with 1.5cm (⅝in) seams. Machine stitch the widths together using a flat fell or French seam.

3 Stitching the hems Turn under and press a double 7.5cm (3in) hem along the lower edge. For a concealed hem, hand slipstitch it in place. Alternatively, straight or blind stitch it on a machine. Turn under and hand or machine stitch a double 2.5cm (1in) hem along each side edge.

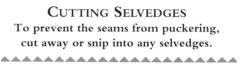

TIP

CUTTING SELVEDGES
To prevent the seams from puckering, cut away or snip into any selvedges.

4 Adding the heading tape Press under the top edge of the curtain to just less than the width of the heading tape. Cut the heading tape to the length of the top edge plus a 2cm (¾in) overlap at either end. Centre the heading tape along the top edge just below the pressed edge and covering the raw edge. Pin the heading tape in place at right angles to the tape length.

5 Neatening the tape ends At the leading edge of the curtains pull the cord ends to the wrong side of the tape and knot them together. Turn under the raw end of the heading tape to just inside the curtain side edge. Pin in place. At the opposite end, pull cords to the right side, then turn in the raw end of the tape and pin. Tack in place.

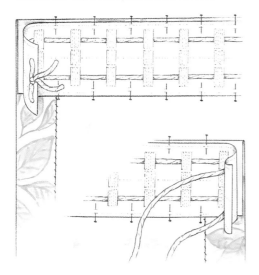

6 Stitching the heading tape Machine stitch the heading tape in place following the marked stitching lines. Stitch the rows in the same direction to prevent the fabric puckering. Stitch across each end of the tape, close to the edge, taking care not to trap the free ends of the cords. Press from the right side.

7 Gathering the curtains Pull up the gathering cords on the heading tape to set in the pleats completely, then ease out the gathers until the curtain top is the required width. Tie the loose cord into a neat bundle or use a curtain tidy. If you are not adding a detachable lining, insert the hooks and hang up the curtain.

◩ *Surprisingly, unlined curtains made up in quite deep colours still allow sunlight to filter into a room. Lovely dappled light effects often result when a patterned fabric is used in this way.*

ADDING A DETACHABLE LINING

A detachable lining allows you to use a lining fabric that requires a different form of cleaning to the main curtain – for instance if you make silk curtains you are unlikely to want the expense and trouble of a silk lining. One option is cotton sateen which comes in a wide range of colours, but if you'd like a little more insulation consider using a thermal lining. Another option is black-out lining which is designed to keep out the light, and which also helps to exclude some external noise and has insulating properties.

◧ *Made into a single unlined curtain, the textured weave of natural linen is shown to full advantage by the light passing through it.*

COTTON TAPE AND FASTENERS

To ensure the lining does not show round the edges of the curtain, fasten the lining and curtain together with tabs of cotton tape and snap fasteners. You need enough cotton tape to stitch a 2.5cm (1in) tab at 40cm (16in) intervals down each side edge, and a snap fastener for each tab.

1 Cutting and stitching the widths Measure the completed unlined curtains. Cut and join widths of lining fabric to this size, less 5cm (2in) on the lower edge, following steps 1 and 2, *Making Unlined Curtains*.

2 Stitching the hems Turn under and press a double 2cm (¾in) hem along the lower and side edges of the lining. Pin and machine stitch the hems in place.

3 Attaching lining tape Measure the the top edge of the lining fabric. Cut a piece of lining tape to this size plus a 2cm (¾in) overlap at either end. Centre the lining tape over the top edge of the lining and pin in place.

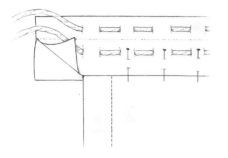

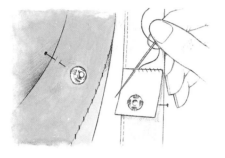

4 Turning in tape ends Deal with the cords as for step 5, *Making Unlined Curtains*. Fold the ends of the tape to the wrong side of lining fabric. Turn under the raw edges and tack in place. Stitch across lower edge and each end of the tape. Slipstitch together the two layers of tape at each end of the top. Pull up the lining tape to match the gathered curtain heading.

5 Marking side edges for fasteners Starting at the base of the curtain heading, use a tape measure and pins to mark 40cm (16in) intervals along both side hems. Repeat to mark corresponding intervals on the lining.

6 Adding tape and fasteners Cut the cotton tape into tabs 2.5cm (1in) long. Stitch one half of a snap fastener to the end of each tab. Position the opposite end of each tab to one of the pinned marks placed along the lining side hems and stitch in place. Handstitch the other halves of the snap fasteners to the corresponding pins on the curtain side hems.

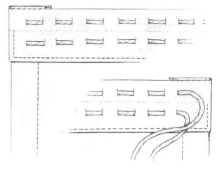

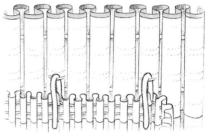

7 Hanging curtain and lining Refit the curtain hooks through the lining tape and then through the curtain heading tape. Press the snap fastener sections together and hang up the lined curtains.

◀ *For pure luxury, few fibres can beat the beauty and lustre of silk. If you invest in silk curtains, make sure you protect them from the destructive effect of sunlight, which weakens the silk, by adding a lining. A detachable lining, which you can wash rather than have dry cleaned, is a convenient and economical option.*

Making curtains

Precise measuring up and cutting out are the crucial first steps to sewing curtains that hang well.

Your choice of curtain style will depend largely on the size and shape of your window, other soft furnishings in the room and the visual effect you want to create. This guide to measuring up can be used for all straight-fall, fabric curtains, lined or unlined, made with tape headings. (Available by the metre or yard from fabric departments, heading tapes are attached to the top of the curtains as the quickest and easiest way of pleating and hanging them.)

You need the following information to calculate the total fabric required to make curtains for a window:

♦ **The width of the curtain track or pole**
♦ **The finished gathered width of each curtain**
♦ **The fabric requirement of the curtain heading tape**
♦ **The desired curtain length**
♦ **The pattern repeat**

TIP

RELIABLE RULE
If possible, use a retractable steel tape rather than a dressmaker's tape to measure the dimensions of the window. A steel tape is longer and will give a much more accurate measurement.

Curtain track or pole

Before measuring up for curtains, fix the track or pole you plan to use in place so that its exact height and width can be measured. As a guide, fix the track or pole between 7.5-12.5cm (3-5in) above the window and allow at least 15cm (6in) overlap on each side, unless it is in a recess, so that the curtain can be swept back away from the window to let in maximum light.

Curtain width

First, simply measure the length of the track or pole and divide this measurement by two for a pair of curtains. For certain tracks, you will have to add extra fabric for an overlap between the two curtains in the centre, so check the instructions with the track.

Heading tape

Now, choose the heading tape you want to use – you will need to know this before you can work out the final fabric amounts because the gathering allowance for different styles of heading tape varies, as the chart to the right shows. As a general guide, you will need at least 1½-2 times the width of the curtain to achieve the necessary fullness.

Curtain length

There are three popular curtain lengths:

Sill length (A) – the curtain hems are 1cm (⅜in) above the sill so that they sweep clear of it.

Below the sill (B) – the curtains hang best if they are between 10 and 15cm (4-6in) below the sill.

Floor length (C) – the curtain hems are 1cm (⅜in) above the floor to prevent wear.

For the curtain length, measure from the top of the fixed curtain track, or from the base of the rings on the curtain pole, to the desired position of the lower edge of the curtain. Ignore heading seam and hem allowances at this stage; they are added on later when calculating fabric quantity.

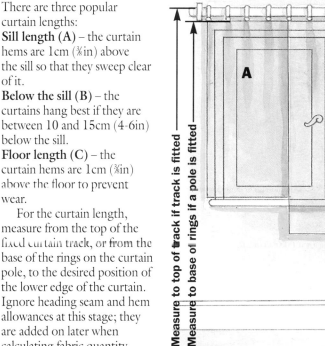

Measure to top of track if track is fitted
Measure to base of rings if a pole is fitted

Heading tape	Fabric needed		
Standard tape	1½-2	x	
Pencil pleat tape	2½-3	x	
Triple pleat	2	x	
Cartridge pleat	2	x	Gathered
Box pleat	3	x	curtain
Goblet pleat	2	x	width
Smocked tape	2	x	

This curtain is gathered using a pencil pleat tape. The ungathered fabric was 2½ -3 times wider than its finished gathered width.

Pattern repeat

For patterned fabrics, you will need to buy extra so that you can match up the pattern across the width and when the curtains are drawn together. Make allowances, too, for any overlap between the closed curtains. To work out the extra fabric required, you have to know the pattern repeat.

To find the pattern repeat allowance, measure the distance (**R**) along the selvedge edge between one pattern motif and the same point on the next identical one. This is often quoted on furnishing fabric details, so look out for it when you are choosing the fabric. As a general guideline, add one extra pattern repeat for every fabric width required.

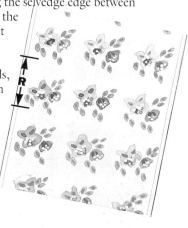

Calculating fabric quantity

The chart below shows how to work out the total amount of fabric needed. The example given here is for curtains, 2m (6⅔ft) long, with a triple pleat tape heading; fill in the blank parts of the chart to calculate the amount of fabric you will need to make curtains for your window. You may find a pocket calculator helpful.

Make sure you always use accurate measurements and measure up all windows separately even if they look identical.

Loosening up

Only work with full and half fabric widths. If your calculations fall the odd bit over a convenient width, ease off the gathering on the heading tape slightly, rather than add another half width of the fabric.

Curtain length	Example cm	in	Your window cm	in
Length of each curtain	200	80		
+ Hem (for 7.5cm/3in deep hem)	12.5	5	12.5	5
+ Heading seam	1.5	⅝	1.5	⅝
+ Pattern repeat	40	16		
Total cut length	**254**	**101⅝**		
Curtain width	**cm**	**in**	**cm**	**in**
Gathered width of each curtain	85	34		
x Allowance for gathering (see heading tape chart)	2			
+ Side hems	10	4	10	4
* Total width for each curtain (add overlap allowance if applicable)	180	72		
÷ Sold fabric width	122	48		
So Number of fabric widths per curtain needed		1½		
x Number of curtains		2		
= Total number of widths		**3**		
Total fabric needed				
Total cut length	254	102		
x Total number of widths		3		
= Total fabric length	762	306		
SO BUY:	**7.8m**	**8½yd**		

* Note: If you need more than one full fabric width to make up the ungathered curtain width, remember to include extra seam allowances.

Cutting out

Find a large flat surface – a clean floor is ideal – that will take the complete curtain length and width. For matching patterned fabrics, you also need to be able to lay two widths side by side.

1 Preparing to cut Lay the fabric flat, right side up. On patterned fabrics, plan, then mark the position of the base; for the best effect, the complete pattern, or a clear section of it, should sit along the base of the curtain after the hem has been turned up.

2 Straightening up the base edge Use a ring binder or a large set square to mark the base edge at right angles out from the selvedge. Then cut the fabric along the marked line.

3 Cutting out Measure the curtain length up from the base edge and, again using your binder or a large set square and ruler, mark the top edge and cut along it. To cut the second length, place the uncut fabric against the cut length and match any pattern design across the two pieces. Cut remaining lengths in the same way.

Joining widths

You may need to join lengths of fabric together to make the total ungathered width for each curtain. If the curtain contains full widths and a half, place the half width on the outer edge.

1 Joining widths Pin the fabric widths together, right sides facing, and then look on the right side to check that the pattern matches. To be sure of an exact match, hold the lengths together using ladder stitch.

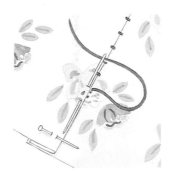

2 Stitching widths Machine stitch the widths together taking a 1.5cm (⅝in) seam allowance. Press the seams to one side, trim to 6mm (¼in), then neaten them with zigzag stitch and remove any ladder stitching. Alternatively, for unlined curtains you can use a French seam.

TIP

The pattern repeat on some fabrics can be quite large, so after cutting out your curtain widths use spare pieces of fabric to make matching tiebacks or scatter cushions.

Curtain glossary

An A-Z of window treatments and terms used in curtain making.

The following pages describe and illustrate the wide variety of window treatments and some of the terms associated with windows that you are likely to come across when making window dressings.

Arched edge Decorative edge shaped like an arch to rise in the middle.

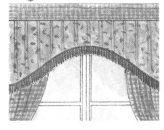

Architrave (Trim) Wooden surround to window or door.
Asymmetrical curtain Curtain draped to one side of a window or of uneven length at either side of a window.

Austrian blind (balloon blind) Soft fabric blind with some fullness, gathered to form ruched swags at base.

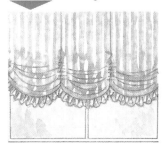

Bay window An angular projection of a house front filled by a window.

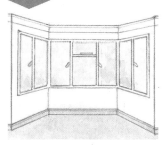

Bishop sleeve curtains Curtains with extra finished length so they billow out over tiebacks when pulled up.

Bow window A curved projection of a house front filled by a window.

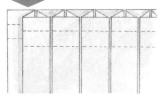

Box pleats Flat pressed symmetrical pleats with fabric folded to back on both sides so adjoining side edges meet.

Brackets Supports for fixing curtain poles, rods and tracks to the wall.

Café curtain Curtain set on a narrow café rod halfway down the window, usually with a *slot* or *scalloped heading*.

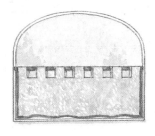

Cartridge pleats Curtain heading with rows of large cylindrical pleats.

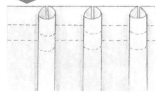

Casement curtain Curtain with a casing at top and bottom fixed on rods.

Casement window Window that opens on vertical hinges.

Castellated edge Decorative edge shaped with square indentations.

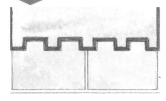

Choux rosette Decoration formed by pulling fabric through a ring into a soft pouffe resembling a cabbage (hence 'choux').

Cleats Hooked fitting beside the window to anchor blind cords when raised.
Cross-over curtains Curtains draped across a window and held back at opposite sides.

Cut drop Cut length of curtain with allowances for heading and hem turnings.

Deadlight The space between the top of the window and the ceiling.
Dormer window A small window that projects from a sloping roof.

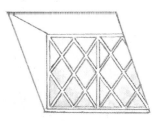

Dress curtains Curtains which are fixed in place so they cannot be drawn.

End stop Fixture at end of track or pole to prevent gliders or rings falling off.

Fascia Thin pelmet (cornice) board covered in fabric or painted. Covers a blind or curtain heading and track.

French window A window which reaches to the floor and opens like a door to provide access to the outside.

Hold back Decorative projection in wood or metal which the curtains are tucked behind to hold them open, away from the window.

Italian stringing Method of holding a curtain open by rings and cord set diagonally across curtain width.

Festoon blind Soft fabric blind permanently gathered into shallow swags that run down the whole length of the blind.

Finial Decorative *end-stop* on curtain pole.

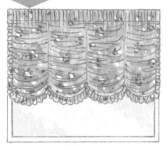

Finished length Length of a finished curtain.
Flemish heading *Goblet pleats* trimmed with rope or furnishing cord, looped and knotted at base of pleats.

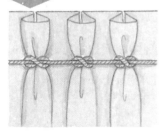

French pleats (pinch pleats) Hand-sewn *triple pleat* curtain heading in which three folds of fabric are pinched together.

Fullness Additional length or width of fabric to allow for drapes, gathers, pleats or swags in a curtain.

Gathered heading Basic gathered heading formed by a narrow heading tape.

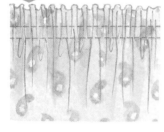

Gliders Runners that fit into and slide along the curtain track to carry curtains.

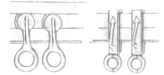

Goblet pleats Formal curtain heading of large cylindrical pleats pinched at the base to form goblet shapes.

Half drop With diagonal patterns allow half the pattern drop as the repeat.
Heading tape Tape attached to the curtain which pulls up to form gathers or pleats.
Hem weight Lead weight sewn into the curtain hem and seams to prevent the curtain puckering at the seams.

Hook drop Measurement from the eye of the curtain hook to the floor.
Hour-glass curtain A *casement curtain* held taut on a rod at top and bottom, and drawn in at the centre forming an hour-glass shape.

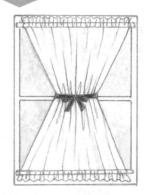

Interlining Soft layer between curtain fabric and lining to give weight and substance, provide insulation, and block light and noise.
Inverted pleat (kick pleat) Reversed *box pleat* with edges of pleat meeting in middle on right side of fabric.

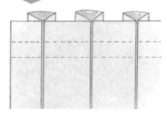

Inverted scallop edge Decorative edge shaped with half-circle indentations.

Lambrequin A stiff, shaped surround to a window, continuing down the sides of the frame.

Lath and fascia Arrangement of *pelmet lath*, *fascia* and *track* which allows heading to be visible but conceals track when curtains are open.

Leading edge Edge of curtain facing into centre of window.
Lead-weighted tape Small lead weights slotted into a tape, used to weight the hems of fine fabrics.
Lining Layer of fabric sewn to the back of curtain to protect it from light, improve insulation and way it hangs.
London blind (flat blind) Soft fabric blind that when raised has a loose swag effect at the base.

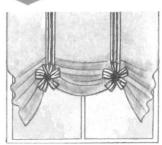

Maltese cross rosette A decorative feature formed by two loops of fabric pressed flat and placed across each other at right angles then secured together.

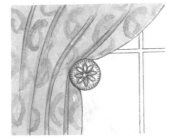

Ombra (embrace) A decorative projection in wood or metal used for holding curtains to the side of the window.

Overlap The point where the curtains meet and cross over by approximately 7.5cm (3in) in the middle of the track or pole.

Oversail The amount by which a pole or track extends on either side beyond the width of the window.

Pattern repeat The distance covered by a fabric design before it repeats itself, usually measured on the length for estimating purposes.

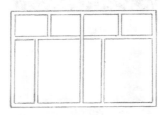

Pelmet (cornice) A decorative surround to conceal curtain *track* and *heading*; can be flat and shaped, often attached to a pelmet box. Alternatively, it is a soft *valance* gathered on to a pole or track.

Pencil pleats A tape or hand sewn curtain heading formed by vertical rows of narrow, densely packed folds.

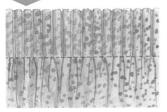

Picture window A large window with wide panes of glass usually placed so that it overlooks a view.

Pin hooks S-shaped curtain hooks with sharpened end for pushing into curtain heading.
Pinch pleats See *French pleats*.
Plastic-covered wire Wire cased in plastic with hooks or screw eyes at the ends to support a lightweight slot-headed curtain.

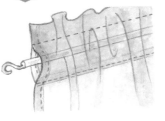

Pleated rosette Decorative feature formed by tightly and evenly pleating a band of fabric into a circular fan shape.

Pleater hooks Curtain hooks used with a cordless heading tape in which the forks of the hook fit into slots in the tape to form the curtain pleats.

Pole A sturdy wooden, metal or plastic bar used with curtain rings to hang medium to heavyweight curtains.

Portière rod A rod to hold a curtain at an external door, with a hinged end that lifts up as the door is opened.

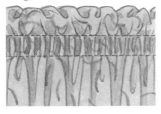

Puffball heading A deep stand-up at the top of a curtain, which is puffed up.

Reefing line A row of rings sewn to the back of a curtain or blind which carries the cord to raise or lower the curtain.

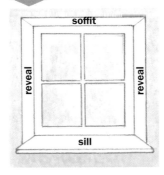

Return The sides of a curtain, valance or pelmet which project out at right angles to the wall.
Reveal The depth of a wall or window frame recess on each side of a window.

Rod A narrow metal or plastic bar used to hang lighter weight curtains.

Roller blind A flat shade that rolls up around a cylinder at the top of the window.

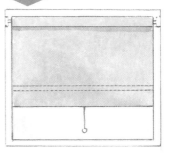

Roman blind Corded blind with base rod and sometimes more rods set horizontally across the back forming straight folds when blind is pulled up.

Rose A decorative feature formed by gathering and twisting fabric to form a rose-like shape.

Sail blind A flat fabric shade secured to the window frame at all four corners with screw-in hooks and eyelets.
Sash window A window with a vertically sliding frame rather than hinges.

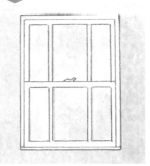

Scalloped edge A decorative edge, shaped with regular semicircular protrusions.

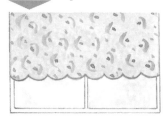

Scalloped heading The scalloped top edge of a curtain with rings or hooks attached to the scallops.

Self-adhesive fabric stiffener Iron-on pelmet interfacing used to stiffen fabric.
Serpentine edge A decorative edge shaped with wavy curves.

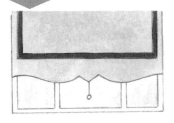

Sew-on hooks Traditional curtain hooks sewn on to gathered or pleated headings.

Sheer curtains/blinds Translucent window dressing made of very lightweight, opaque fabric which provides privacy without blocking light.
Sill A horizontal ledge at base of window (see *Reveal*)
Sky light A window set into a roof or ceiling to provide overhead lighting.

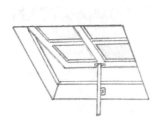

Slot heading (case heading) A stitched, tube-like heading at the top edge of a curtain, which the rod or pole is pushed through.

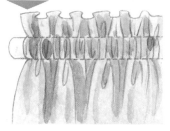

Soffit The upper plane of a window opening, at right-angles to the wall, above the window (see *Reveal*).
Smocked heading A *pencil pleat heading* stitched to create a honeycomb effect.

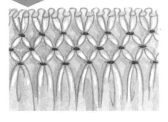

Spring clips Decorative curtain rings to thread over rods or poles, with clip attachments that grip the top edge of light or sheer curtains.

Stand-up The part of the curtain extending above the *suspension point*.
Suspension point The line along top edge of the curtain, below which the fabric is hanging (see *Stand-up*).
Swag A length of fabric which has been arranged to hang in sweeping folds above a window or bed.

Tab headings An open curtain heading in which the curtain hangs below a pole or rod suspended by fabric loops or ties.

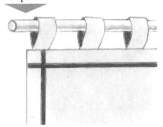

Tail Folded or pleated fabric arranged to fall in vertical folds between or at the ends of *swags* (see *Swag*).
Tension rod A fine plastic rod with an internal spring mechanism to hold it in place across the window recess, often used for café curtains.
Thermal lining (Milium) Interlining with an insulating aluminium backing.
Tie-back A shaped and stiffened band, plait, tasselled cord etc, to hold curtains to the side of a window.

Track A plastic or metal curtain rail with fitted *gliders*.
Trefoil A double pleat used for accent in a valance.

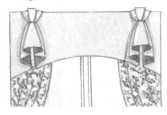

Triple pleats See *French pleats*.
Trumpet A conical pleat used for accent in a valance.

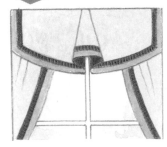

Tudor ruff heading A curtain heading with a tightly gathered, smocked shape.

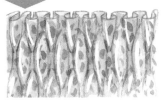

Unlined curtain A single thickness curtain that does not block out too much light.

Valance A soft fabric pelmet with a gathered or flat skirt hanging at the top of the window to conceal the track.

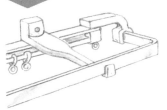

Valance rail A fixture projecting from the front of either a curtain track or pole to carry a *valance* in front of the curtain.

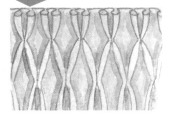

Vogue heading A curtain heading with staggered pinched pleats.

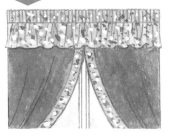

Zigzag A decorative edge cut into sharp triangular-shaped points.

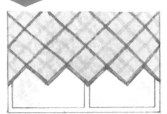

FORMAL BOLSTER COVER

A bolster cushion provides a contrast in style to other cushions in your sitting room or bedroom. This version is finished at each end with a gathered panel neatened with bold buttons.

B olsters are round, elongated cushions that are typically used on beds, day beds, sofas or chaise longues. On beds, bolsters give support to other cushions or pillows, but they can be used in their own right as very distinctive accessories for other soft furnishings round the home.

Bolsters can be covered to match or contrast with their surroundings, and are made in a range of fabrics from rich velvets to pretty broderie anglaise or coarse natural cloth.

Bolster covers can be made in several different ways – the one shown here has gathered ends that are finished with a decorative trim such as a covered button, tassel or rosette.

Two neatly trimmed bolsters make comfortable armrests at each end of a day bed.

MAKING THE COVER

Bolster pads come in a range of sizes from department stores, or can be made to order.

▶ See pages 11-12 for details about piping.

1 Cutting out the body Cut a piece of fabric equal to the length (**A**) by the circumference (**B**) of the bolster pad, plus 1.5cm (⅝in) seam allowance all round. (Unless the bolster is exceptionally fat, the end pieces can be cut from the remaining width; if in doubt make a cutting plan before buying fabric.)

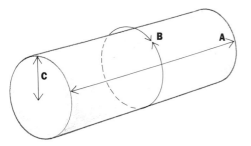

2 Cutting the ends Cut two rectangles of bolster fabric equal to the circumference (**B**) by the radius (**C**), plus 1.5cm (⅝in) all round. These can be cut across the width or length of the fabric, depending on the way you want the pattern to run.

3 Making up the body With right sides together, fold the main piece in half lengthways. Stitch down the length of the seam, taking a 1.5cm (⅝in) allowance, leaving an opening in the centre for the zip. Hold the seam closed with tacking and press open. Centre the zip face down over the seam, and tack down each side, 1cm (⅜in) from seam. Machine or hand stitch zip in place, stitching down each side and across both ends. Remove tacking and turn right side out.

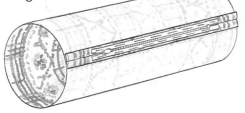

▼ A brightly patterned fabric and extra large self-cover buttons give these bolsters a thoroughly modern image.

4 Preparing the ends With right sides together, stitch along the short edges of each end piece, taking a 1.5cm (⅝in) seam allowance. Press the seams open. Turn under a 1.5cm (⅝in) hem on one long edge of each end piece and press. Using strong thread, work two rows of gathering stitches by hand or machine, close to the pressed edges.

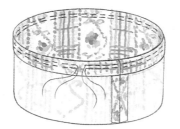

6 Attaching the ends Slip an end piece over one end of the main body tube, with right sides together and matching raw edges. Pin, tack and stitch, using zipper foot. Clip and grade seam allowances, and press them towards the end. Repeat to attach the other end piece.

7 Finishing the ends Insert the bolster pad through one end of the cover so its ends align with the piping. Gather at one end and fasten the threads. Repeat at the other end. Cover two self-cover buttons, following manufacturer's instructions, and stitch over gathers at each end.

▲ Covering this bolster in a bright blue version of the cushion fabric gives the whole scheme a well coordinated boost.

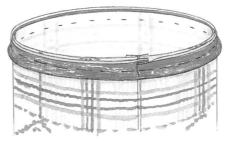

5 Adding the piping Make up two lengths of contrast piping, each long enough to fit round the circumference of the bolster, plus 4cm (1½in) for joining. Pin and tack the piping round both ends of the main body, matching the raw edges together, and butt join the ends. Stitch in place using a zipper foot.

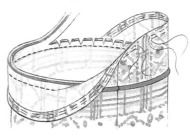

FLANGED COVERS

Frame plain cushion covers with a border of fabric. The border – or flanged edge – adds decorative impact without the need for extra trims.

F langed cushion covers can be made in two ways, either with a separate border of contrasting fabric or an integrated flange of the same fabric as the cover itself, which is called a self border. The self border cover is brilliantly simple to make – you just cut a panel of fabric larger than the cushion pad, make up the cover in the usual way, then top stitch the two layers together to form a border.

Making a separate border is slightly more time consuming, but presents the opportunity to display a splendid design in the border, or to combine two different fabrics. Try pairing a check with a floral, a plain with a print, or even two different plains – the only limitation is that the fabrics should be the same weight.

BASIC FLANGED COVER

YOU WILL NEED

- ❖ FABRIC (for amounts see steps 1 and 2)
- ❖ SQUARE PILLOW PAD
- ❖ ZIP – 5cm (2in) less than pad size
- ❖ MATCHING SEWING THREAD
- ❖ RULER AND CHALK

Make up this cover with a centred zip opening on the back, using a light to mediumweight crisp furnishing fabric such as cotton. The inner panel can be formed with straight stitching or, for a more decorative and sturdy effect, machine satin stitch. The instructions are for a square cover, so choose a square pad – for the best effect it should be nice and plump.

TIP

MACHINE SATIN STITCH
To work a smooth satin stitch, stitch the seam twice. First set the machine to an open zigzag and stitch along the panel lines. Then set the machine to a tight zigzag and stitch over the first row.

◀ *Flanged cushion covers are equally at home in a living room or bedroom. Make them up in a range of coordinating fabrics for a mood setting collection.*

SIMPLE MITRED FLANGE

A step in between the basic flanged cover and a cover with a separate border, this method allows you to add a border in a contrasting fabric, or make a feature of the pattern as shown on the previous page.

YOU WILL NEED

- ❖ MAIN FABRIC
- ❖ CONTRAST FABRIC, or panel from main fabric
- ❖ SQUARE PILLOW PAD
- ❖ ZIP
- ❖ MATCHING THREAD
- ❖ RULER AND CHALK

1 Cutting out and stitching Follow steps 1-3 *Basic Flanged Cover*, to cut out the front and back panels and make up the back.

2 Cutting border Cut four strips 7.5cm (3in) wide by length of square from contrast fabric. Press under 1.25cm (½in) on one long edge of each panel.

3 Adding panels Right sides up, and matching raw edges, position a panel to opposite sides of front cover and pin. Pin a panel to remaining sides, folding in each raw end to form a mitre. Press mitre and trim seam to 1.25cm (½in). Tack panels in place, then machine stitch each mitre close to folded edge, stitching through both border and cover.

1 Cutting out the front Measure the pillow pad and add 12.5cm (5in). Cut out one square to this amount. This will allow for a 5cm (2in) flange and a seam allowance of 1.25cm (½in).

2 Cutting out the back Using the front folded in half as a pattern, cut out two back panels, adding a seam allowance of 2cm (¾in) on one long edge of each panel.

3 Adding the zip Stitch backs together for 9cm (3½in) at each end, with 2cm (¾in) seams. Tack seam closed and press allowances open. Centre zip on seam and machine stitch either side.

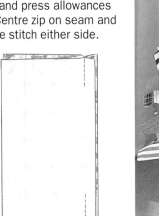

4 Stitching cover With right sides together, stitch outer edge, taking a 1.25cm (½in) seam. Clip corners. Turn cover to right side. Press, ensuring that seam runs along edge.

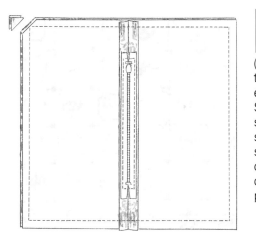

5 Stitching border panel Using chalk and a ruler, draw a square 5cm (2in) in from outer edge. Pin, then tack inner square, ensuring border lies flat. Stitch using either a straight stitch or a machine satin stitch. To avoid distortion, start stitching from the centre of a side, not a corner. Remove tacking, press cover and insert pad.

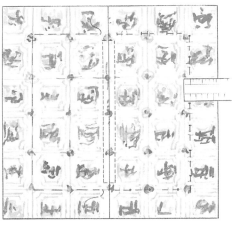

▶ *Vivid pink and red checks paired with a bold floral pattern illustrate a successful choice of two fabrics for the cover.*

4 Joining cover With right sides together, stitch front to back taking a 1.25cm (½in) seam while catching in border. Clip across corners and turn cover to right side through zip opening. Press. Form inner panel by tacking, then stitching close to folded edge, through all layers.

SEPARATE BORDER COVER

Made with a separate border, mitred at each corner, this cover can be closed with a zip or buttons for a more decorative effect. The border is inserted into the cover seam, so it is important to stitch the corners with care to ensure a defined shape.

1 Making a pattern Measure the pillow pad and draw a square the same size. Draw a second square, 5cm (2in) out from first square. Draw two lines diagonally from corner to corner. Carefully cut away one of the side border sections, then cut out the centre square.

2 Cutting out the front and borders Adding 1.25cm (½in) to the outer edges of all pieces for seams, cut one square from the main fabric and eight border sections from the contrasting fabric.

❒ *The button closure works particularly well with the subtle shirting fabric which is used to make these cushion covers.*

3 Cutting the back Using the front panel folded in half as a pattern, cut two back panels adding a 5cm (2in) hem to the long edge of each panel. The panels overlap by 2cm (¾in) to form a button extension.

5 Joining back panels With right sides up, position the buttonhole panel so it overlaps second panel by 2cm (¾in) and pin. To secure, stitch close to the folded edge of top layer for about 6cm (2¼in) then across to the seam.

4 Neatening back panels Press under and stitch a double 2cm (¾in) hem on one long edge of each back panel. Work three buttonholes lengthways in hem of one panel, positioning one in the centre and the other two either side of centre.

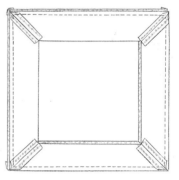

6 Joining borders Right sides together, pin four borders together to form a ring. Stitch taking a 1.25cm (½in) seam, stopping 1.25cm (½in) from inner edge. Repeat with other panels. Right sides together, stitch outer edges of panels. Turn to right side and press.

7 Adding border Position border to right side cushion front with raw edges matching. Tack. Position back cover over border, right side covers together and stitch outer edge. Turn to right side. Stitch on buttons to correspond with buttonholes and insert pad.

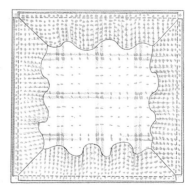

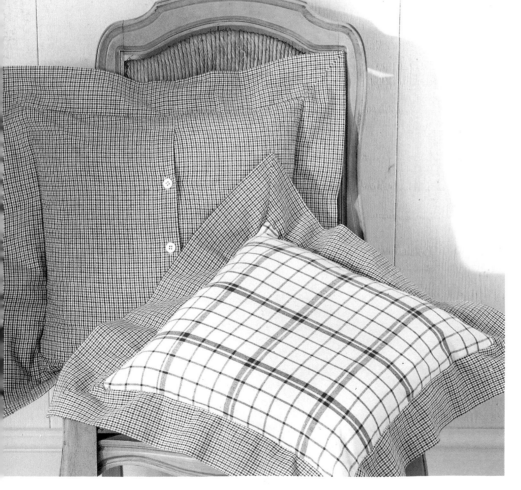

FRILLED CUSHION COVERS

*Give square or round cushion covers a more luxurious
look with the addition of a double frill, gathered and sewn
between the front and back panels.*

A frilled cushion cover is distinctly feminine, and adds a softening touch to a room. The choice of fabrics affects the look of the cushion – a cover made in a crisp stripe with a striped frill has a restrained charm, while a rose-strewn chintz cover with a contrasting or lacy frill, suggests pure frivolity and romance.

The easiest method of adding a frill to a cushion cover is to use a double frill, so called because it is made with a folded strip of fabric that looks the same on both sides. This type of frill gives the cushion a lovely plump appearance and a very neat finish, with the fold forming the outer edge and the raw edges enclosed in the seam.

Adding piping between the frill and the cushion gives definition to its shape. For an extremely lavish finish, make two frills of slightly different depths in coordinating fabrics and layer them together.

The softening effect of frills gives these cushions an extra plump look and makes this cane seat an altogether more inviting prospect.

SQUARE FRILLED CUSHION COVERS

1 **Cutting out the cover**
Measure the sides of the cushion pad. For the front panel, cut one piece of fabric to these measurements plus 1.5cm (⅝in) seam allowance all round. For back panels, cut two rectangles of fabric the length of one side of the cushion pad, plus 3cm (1¼in), by half the adjacent side, plus 10cm (4in).

YOU WILL NEED
❖ FURNISHING FABRIC
❖ SQUARE CUSHION PAD
❖ TAPE MEASURE
❖ SEWING THREAD

▶ See pages 11-12 for piping, page 32 for French seams and pages 29-30 for frills.

2 **Cutting out the frill** Measure all round the cushion pad and double the measurement. Cut strips across the width of the fabric so that when joined they make up this length, by 20cm (8in) wide. For a fuller or deeper frill, add to the length or the width of the strip respectively.

3 **Preparing the frill** Right sides together, join frill strips into a circle. Press seams open. Wrong sides together, fold fabric in half lengthways and pin raw edges together. Divide the frill in four and mark with pins.

4 **Stitching the gathering** Run rows of gathering stitches 1.2cm (½in) and 2cm (¾in) in from the raw edges of the frill. Stop and start the stitching half way between the pin marks.

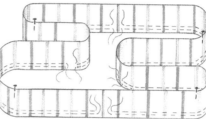

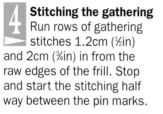

▲ *A piped trim highlights the fabric colours and emphasizes the shape of a frilled cushion cover.*

5 **Attaching the frill** With right sides together and raw edges even, pin the frill round the edge of the front cover panel, matching the pin marks to the corners. Pull up gathering stitches to fit. Adjust the gathers so that they are even, allowing extra fabric at the corners. Machine stitch the frill in place. Snip into the frill seam allowance at each corner.

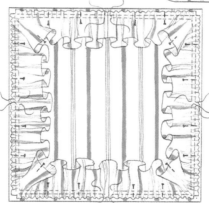

6 **Attaching the cushion back** On one long edge of each back panel turn under and machine stitch a 1.5cm (⅝in) double hem. With right sides together and raw edges even, place the two back panels on the front cover panel so that the hemmed edges overlap. Pin, tack and machine stitch a 1.5cm (⅝in) seam all round the outer edge, through all layers.

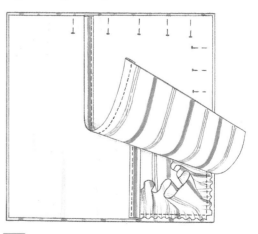

ROUND FRILLED CUSHION COVERS

1. For the cushion cover, cut one circle of fabric the size of the cushion pad plus a 1.5cm (⅝in) seam allowance all round. Use this circle as a template for cutting the two back panels as follows. Fold the circle in half and then ease open folded edge to add an extra 10cm (4in) from the straight edge as shown (right). Cut two pieces of fabric to this size, taking care to match directional patterns.
2. For positioning marks, fold the front circle of fabric into quarters and mark the edge of each fold with a pin.

3. To make up the round cover, follow steps 2-7 of Square Frilled Cushion Cover. When joining frill to front cover panel, match the sections to the pin marks.

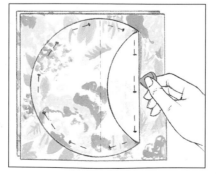

7 **Finishing the cushion** Trim seams and clip corners to reduce bulk and turn cover to the right side. Insert cushion pad and hand stitch the back flap closed. Alternatively, handstitch circles of touch-and-close fastening between the back panels of the cushion cover.

A guide to cushion pads

When you can't find the right size or shape of cushion pad, you can always make your own to suit your needs.

Cushion pads can be quickly made when necessary, to suit odd shapes and sizes. They can be made from a variety of fabrics such as calico, cambric, ticking, lining fabric or an oddment of sheeting or cotton fabric. For hard-wearing cushions, choose a firmly woven fabric that will keep its shape; when using a feather and down filling, the pad must be made from downproof ticking.

Cushions get their shapes from ready-made pads or loose fillings. Depending on their washability, loose fillings can either be stuffed directly into the cushion cover, or encased in a separate pad for easy removal.

Fillings for cushion pads

Choose the filling for your cushion pad to suit the position and purpose of the cushion. There is a range of natural and manmade materials:

Feather
A traditional and widely used filling, feathers are expensive but they make soft, luxurious cushions that can be quickly plumped into shape. They can be mixed with down or recycled from old cushion pads. Team a feather filling with downproof cambric – this is waxed on the wrong side to stop the feathers from working through.

Down
Down is the very soft underfeathers of birds. It is very light but also expensive, and makes a good filling for fine fabrics such as silk.

Kapok
An old fashioned filling, kapok is an inexpensive natural vegetable fibre that is widely available. Pads made from kapok have a similar look and feel to feather pads, but they tend to lose their shape more readily. Since kapok cannot be washed, it has been largely superseded by more durable manmade fillings.

Synthetic fibre fill
Synthetic fibre fillings are often used in place of natural materials. They are an inexpensive alternative to feathers but the cushion pad will not plump up so well. The pad cover can be made up from a cotton or calico fabric. Synthetic fillings are washable and hypo-allergenic.

Wadding
Made from synthetic or natural cotton fibres bonded together, wadding makes a light washable filling. Available in several thicknesses (weights), a cushion pad will have to be made up of several layers.

Foam
There are three different types of foam filling: solid foam block, foam chips or shredded foam. Use *solid foam block* for making gusset and sofa cushions. Available in several densities depending on the firmness you prefer, all can be cut to awkward shapes with a bread knife. A foam block needs an inner cover to contain it, as the foam crumbles with time. To round off the foam edges wrap the block in a layer of thin wadding. *Foam chips* are the cheapest filling for a cushion pad. They can look lumpy, so wrap in wadding for a smooth look. *Shredded foam* is a smoother version of foam chips.

Polystyrene granules
These small expanded polystyrene beads are usually used for large floor cushions or bean bags. They move about inside the cushion pad to mould round the sitter, providing comfortable support. You need approximately 2.7kg (6lb) to fill a standard size bean bag – buy spare beads as they flatten with use, and need to be topped up.

feather

kapok

synthetic fibre fill

wadding

synthetic fibre fill

solid foam

kapok

Making a knife-edge cushion pad

1 Cutting out From fabric, cut out a front and back 2.5cm (1in) larger all round than finished cushion size. Fold front into quarters. Mark a point halfway along each open side. Mark 1.2cm (½in) diagonally in from the open corner.

Amounts of filling required

For an average size pad 35-38cm (14-15in) square:
1kg (2¼lb) feathers; or ½kg (1lb) down
½kg (1lb) kapok
½kg (1lb) synthetic fibre fill
Several layers of wadding, cut to size

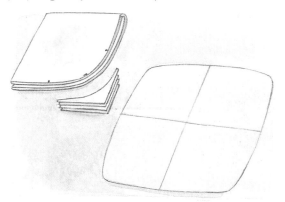

2 Shaping cover Trim through all layers starting from the side centre to the 1.2cm (½in) mark, then round to the centre side on opposite edge. Unfold front and use it as a template for shaping the back to match the front.

3 Stitching cover Right sides together, pin and machine stitch front to back, taking 1.5cm (⅝in) seam and leaving a central opening in one side. (Use a French seam for feather or down fillings.) Back stitch across either end of opening.

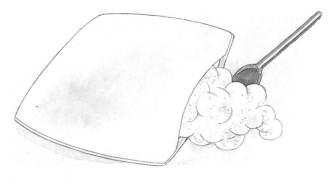

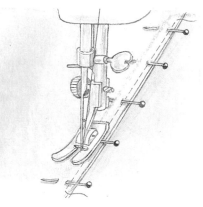

4 Filling the cover Trim corners and turn cover right side out. Press under seam allowance on either side of opening. Fill with the chosen filling, working it well into the corners using a blunt tool such as a wooden spoon.

5 Finishing cover When the pad is nicely rounded, pin opening closed. Edgestitch across the opening. On a feather or down pad edgestitch entire edge.

Ready-made pads

Square, round, rectangular or bolster shaped cushion pads are readily available as well as some unusual shapes such as hearts. These pads can be purchased with a variety of fillings.

Feather pads

Square pads are available in 30cm (12in), 35cm (14in), 38cm (15in), 40cm (16in), 45cm (18in), 50cm (20in), 55cm (22in), 60cm (24in), 68cm (27in), 76cm (30in) and 91cm (36in) squares.

Rectangular pads come in sizes 30 x 55cm (12 x 22in), 30 x 40cm (12 x 16in), 35 x 45cm (14 x 18in) and 60 x 40cm (24 x 16in).

Round pads come with a 5cm (2in) deep gusset. Sizes are 38cm (15in) and 45cm (28in) in diameter.

Bolster pads are generally 45cm (18in) long with 17cm (7in) diameter ends.

Duck down and feather pads

Square pads are available in 30cm (12in), 38cm (15in), 40cm (16in) and 50cm (20in) squares.

Synthetic polyester pads

Square pads are available in 35cm (14in), 38cm (15in), 40cm (16in) and 50cm (20in) squares.

CIRCULAR TABLE CLOTHS

Round tables, however ordinary, instantly take on an air of distinction when covered with an easy-to-make circular cloth. It's a soft look that's particularly appropriate for a bedside table.

C overing a round table with a cloth is an ideal way of introducing a new fabric into a scheme and adding the softening effect of extra drapery. It's also an economical solution for hiding an old table so that it can play a new role as an occasional table in the living room or as a bedside table.

You may already have a round table that has seen better days, or you can hunt for a suitable candidate in a secondhand shop. Alternatively, buy a self-assembly, chipboard version, designed to be covered with a cloth.

Such tables are inexpensive and readily available in a range of diameters from stores or by mail order from magazines.

You can make a round table cloth to cover a table of any size. For a large cloth, you may want to avoid the extra expense of lining it, although a lining does give the finished cloth extra body and a more luxurious appearance. The cloth must hang to the floor if it is to hide the table underneath. You can lengthen shorter cloths by trimming them with a frill, deep fringe or braid.

A crisp glazed chintz in a fresh, rose print makes an attractive and elegant cloth for this bedside table. A disc of glass cut to fit the table top ensures that you can put the table to good use while maintaining its smart appearance.

MAKING A BASIC CIRCULAR CLOTH

The simplest circular cloth is cut from a square of fabric and hemmed. Add a lining for a fuller, more luxurious look to the skirt and to give extra protection to the table surface.

ESTIMATING FABRIC AMOUNTS

To estimate how much fabric you need, calculate the required diameter of the cloth. Measure the diameter of the table top and add twice the overhang plus allowances (see Step 1). Allow enough fabric to cut a square with sides equal to this measurement. For most cloths you need more than one width of fabric. To avoid a centre seam join panels of fabric on either side of a central panel. Check the width of your fabric. If the diameter of the cloth is between one and one and a half fabric widths, you need a length of fabric double the diameter. If the diameter of the cloth is more than one and a half fabric widths, you need a fabric length triple the diameter.

◣ *When joining fabric widths, ensure the seams are on each side of a central panel.*

1 Measuring cloth diameter Decide on the overhang of the basic table cloth. Measure the diameter of the table (**A**), plus twice the overhang (**B**). Add to this measurement 4cm (1½in) for the hem allowance and a 1.5cm (⅝in) seam allowance for each panel edge that has to be joined.

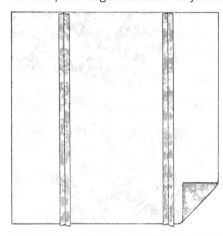

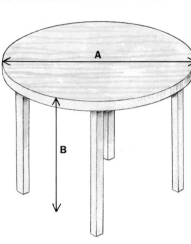

2 Joining widths *For two fabric widths,* cut length in two. Use one piece for centre panel. Cut other piece in half lengthways and, with right sides together, join to either side of central panel. Press seams open. *For three widths,* cut length in three, and join long edges.

3 Preparing paper pattern Fold fabric into quarters matching outer edges and seams. Cut out a square of pattern paper to this size. Working on a surface which can take a drawing pin, push pin into one corner of paper.

4 Drawing circular pattern Wrap one end of a length of string around a pencil and the other end around the drawing pin so that the length of the taut string is the radius of the table cloth. Holding the pencil upright, draw a quarter circle on the pattern paper.

YOU WILL NEED

- ❖ FABRIC
- ❖ TAPE MEASURE
- ❖ PATTERN PAPER
- ❖ DRAWING PIN
- ❖ STRING
- ❖ PENCIL
- ❖ SCISSORS
- ❖ LINING FABRIC (optional)
- ❖ MATCHING THREAD

◪ *A jazzy bullion fringe is an exotic finishing touch to adorn a lavish table cloth in this star-struck fanciful bedroom.*

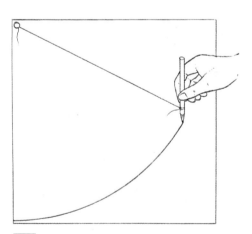

5 Cutting out the fabric Pin the paper pattern to the folded fabric, matching the right angle corner to the centre fabric fold. Cut the fabric, through all thicknesses, along the drawn pattern line. With a bulky or slippery fabric cut through only two layers at once, having tacked the pattern to the fabric. Open out the fabric circle and press flat.

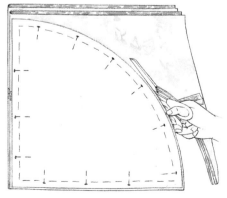

6 Turning up the hem Machine stitch all round the circle 2cm (¾in) from the outer edge. To make sure that the fabric lies flat, snip into seam allowance at regular intervals all round the edge. Press under the hem allowance so that the stitching line falls on the wrong side, close to the fold.

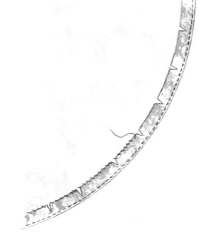

7 Hemming the cloth If the cloth is not going to be lined turn under 6mm (¼in) on the raw edge of the hem. Press and tack. Hand or machine stitch close to the folded edge.

8 Lining the cloth (optional) Omit Step 7. Cut a circle of lining the same size as the fabric and turn up a 2.5cm (1in) hem, as in Step 6. With wrong sides facing, pin fabric and lining together and slipstitch the folded hems together. Press, making sure the lining does not ease round to the right side.

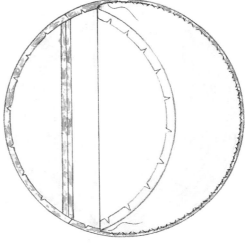

MAKING A RUFFLE-EDGED CLOTH

Adding a ruffle to the basic circular cloth creates a feminine finish and helps to hold out the skirt of the cloth. The ruffle is made from a hemmed strip, in the same or a contrasting fabric, and is topstitched around the edge of the cloth. A ruffled cloth may work out to be a more economical alternative if it allows you to cut the main circle from one width of fabric. Then you can use a coordinating fabric remnant for the ruffle.

1 Measuring up for circular cloth Decide on the depth of the ruffle. Subtract the ruffle depth from the overhang measurement (**B**), and add 2cm (¾in) for the hem. Make a basic circular cloth following the instructions on the previous page.

2 Cutting the ruffle Measure the circumference of the cloth and double the measurement. Cut strips across the width of the fabric to this measurement by the ruffle depth, plus 6cm (2¼in) for the hems.

3 Preparing the ruffle Right sides together, join ends of ruffle strips to form a circle. Neaten, then press seams open. Turn under, press and stitch a 1.5cm (⅝in) double hem along the lower edge. Neaten top edge by pressing under a 3cm (1¼in) hem.

4 Stitching the gathering Run two parallel rows of gathering stitches 1.5cm (⅝in) and 2.5cm (1in) from the folded edge of ruffle ring through both layers. For even gathering, stop and start the stitching at intervals along the length.

5 Marking the ruffle and cloth Fold the cloth in quarters and mark the edge folds with pins. Lay the ruffle flat and fold in half. Mark the four folds with pins on the top edge.

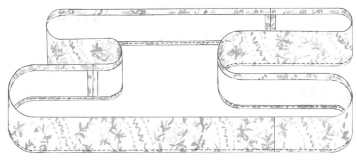

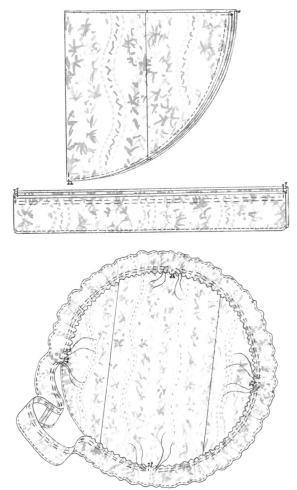

6 Attaching the ruffle Matching marker pins, place wrong side of ruffle on right side of cloth, overlapping ruffle top edge by 3cm (1¼in). Pin the ruffle to the cloth, pulling up the gathering stitches to fit evenly. Working from the front, machine stitch through all layers, between the rows of gathering. Remove gathering threads.

▲ *A generous deep ruffle adds a professional looking finish to the hem of a circular cloth. The addition of a deep frill may also mean that you can cut the cloth from one fabric width.*

BOX-PLEATED TABLE CLOTHS

A box-pleated skirt makes a tailored alternative to gathers for a table cloth, giving a neat, fitted finish. You can either pleat up the whole skirt or just add a smart inverted box pleat at each corner.

Y ou can make a box-pleated table cloth to fit any shape of table top, from a simple square or circle to a curving kidney shape, and you can cut and pleat the skirt in a number of ways to show off the table style and fabric at its best.

On a breakfast or dressing table a short pleated cloth makes a smart yet lighthearted alternative to a standard table cloth, and draws attention to attractive table legs. A floor-length pleated table cloth gives a softly tailored finish as the pleats fan out prettily as they touch the floor, and hide a multitude of sins on a battered dining or occasional table.

There are all sorts of variations – you can position the pleats so that they butt up to each other or leave a space in between; on a square or rectangular table, you can save on fabric by making a straight-sided cloth with an inverted box pleat at each corner.

Certain fabric designs have useful markings which help you line up the pleats, so take advantage of a stripe, check or the edge of a pattern repeat to make pleating easier. Floral patterns also work well, creating a soft contrast to the crisp pleats. Use a medium to heavyweight fabric for firm pleats that hold their shape and check how the fabric pleats before buying.

A box-pleated skirt adds a frivolous finish to this smartly fitted table cloth. The cloth is made by extending the top panel down over the sides of the table, and shaping it with darts at each corner, before adding the skirt.

MAKING A BOX-PLEATED TABLE CLOTH

The best proportion for the box pleats depends on the size and style of the table and on the fabric you choose. As a rough guide, make the box pleats 5-12.5cm (2-5in) wide. To make sure you have whole pleats all round the skirt, choose a width of pleat that divides equally into the length of the table top perimeter. If the length does not divide up equally, it's fairly easy to calculate the exact pleat size.

Measure all round the table top to find the perimeter, and divide this by the approximate pleat size you would like. Round this figure up to the nearest whole number and then divide the perimeter of the table top by this whole number. This gives the actual size of each pleat. On a table with corners try to position the pleats so that they fall on either side of the corners.

YOU WILL NEED

❖ TAPE MEASURE
❖ BROWN PAPER
❖ PINS
❖ FABRIC
❖ PIPING CORD
  for covered piping
❖ MATCHING SEWING
  THREAD
❖ TAILORS' CHALK

▶ For more information on making and attaching piping see pages 11-12.

 Making the table top pattern
Square or rectangular pattern Measure the length and width of the table top and cut a piece of brown paper to this size. *Circular or irregular pattern* Cut a piece of brown paper larger than the table top and lay it over the table. Holding it in place, press all round the edge and then cut along the creases you've made.

▶ *By experimenting with a fabric design you can create interesting effects on a box-pleated table cloth. On this cloth bold stripes are tucked within the box pleats at the table edge to emerge as a splash of colour lower down.*

2 Cutting out the top panel Pin the pattern to the right side of the fabric. Adding a 1.5cm (⅝in) seam allowance all round, cut out the fabric.

3 Cutting out the skirt Measure the drop from the table top to the desired skirt length plus 4.5cm (1¾in) for seam and hem allowances. For the skirt width, measure all round the table top and multiply this measurement by three. Allowing for 1.5cm (⅝in) seams and for pattern matching, cut and join fabric widths to make a continuous loop to the required width and skirt length. Turn up and stitch a double 1.5cm (⅝in) hem along the lower edge.

4 Marking the pleat positions Decide on the pleat width, calculating the exact width as described above, if necessary. Starting at a seamline, use a ruler to divide the upper edge of the skirt into equal sections, each measuring the pleat width. Mark the sections with tailors' chalk.

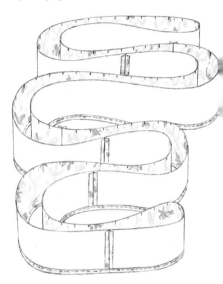

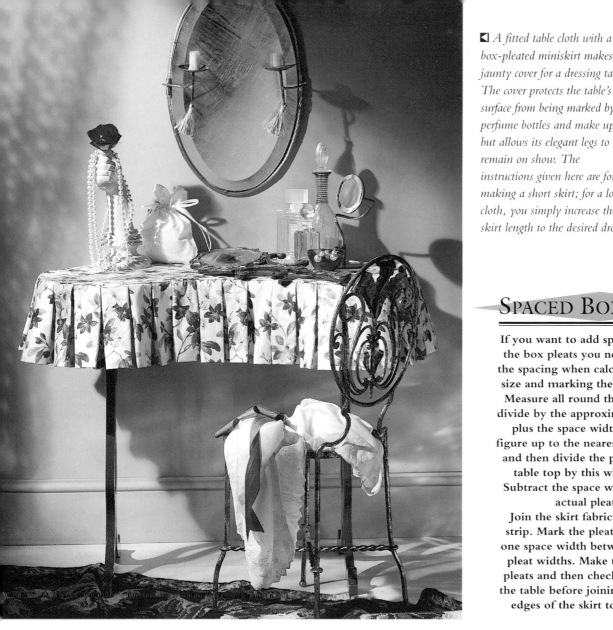

◀ *A fitted table cloth with a box-pleated miniskirt makes a jaunty cover for a dressing table. The cover protects the table's surface from being marked by perfume bottles and make up, but allows its elegant legs to remain on show. The instructions given here are for making a short skirt; for a longer cloth, you simply increase the skirt length to the desired drop.*

SPACED BOX PLEATS

If you want to add spaces in between the box pleats you need to allow for the spacing when calculating the pleat size and marking the pleat positions. Measure all round the table top and divide by the approximate pleat width plus the space width. Round this figure up to the nearest whole number and then divide the perimeter of the table top by this whole number. Subtract the space width to give the actual pleat size.

Join the skirt fabric into one long strip. Mark the pleat positions with one space width between every three pleat widths. Make the spaced box pleats and then check the fit around the table before joining the two short edges of the skirt to form a loop.

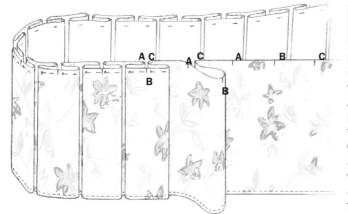

5 Folding the pleats
Three chalk marks (**A**, **B** and **C**) make up each pleat. Working from the right side, fold the fabric with wrong sides together so that **A** and **C** match. Press and pin the fold of fabric flat so that **B** is centred over **A** and **C**. Continue pinning pleats all round the skirt in this way. Check the skirt fits around the table, then tack the pleats in place.

6 Adding piping (optional)
Make up sufficient fabric-covered piping to go all round the edge of the table cloth top panel plus 2.5cm (1in) for overlaps. Matching the raw edges, pin and tack the piping all round the right side of the top panel. At corners and curves, clip into the piping seam allowance for ease.

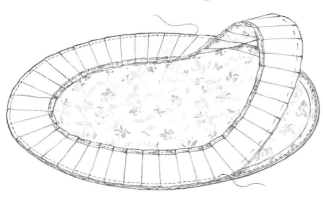

7 Assembling the cloth
With the right sides together, matching the raw edges, pin and tack the box-pleated skirt all round the top panel. On a table with corners, arrange the pleats so they fall on either side of the corners. Using a sewing machine zip foot, stitch through all the layers close to the piping cord.

8 Finishing the table cloth
Grade the seams, press them towards the skirt and neaten them with zigzag stitch. Press the pleats along their whole length to give them a crisp, neat finish; or, for a less formal look, press along the upper edge only.

CORNER-PLEATED TABLE CLOTH

This table cloth is a chic option for a square or rectangular table. It has a straight skirt, with an inverted box pleat at each corner – a style which is very economical on fabric.

The box pleats are held in shape with decorative ties, and each pleat has a separate pleat insert at the back which you can make in a contrast fabric to highlight the pleats. You need the same materials to make this cloth as for the box-pleated version, plus the optional contrast fabric.

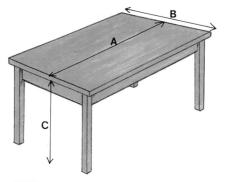

1 **Cutting the top panel** Measure the length (**A**) and width (**B**) of the table top. Cut a piece of main fabric to this size, adding 1.5cm (⅝in) all round for seams.

2 **Cutting the skirt panels** Measure the skirt drop (**C**). Cut two rectangles of fabric measuring **A** plus 23cm (9in) by **C** plus 4.5cm (1¾in). Cut two rectangles of fabric measuring **B** plus 23cm (9in) by **C** plus 4.5cm (1¾in).

3 **Cutting the pleat inserts** Cut four rectangles of main or contrasting fabric, measuring 23cm (9in) by **C** plus 4.5cm (1¾in).

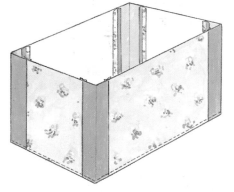

4 **Stitching the skirt** With right sides together, taking 1.5cm (⅝in) seams, pin and stitch the side edges of the skirt and pleat inserts into a loop with an insert at each corner, to correspond to the shape of the table top. Press seams open. Stitch a double 1.5cm (⅝in) hem along the lower edge.

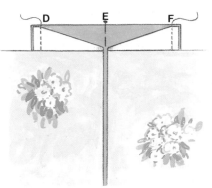

5 **Making the inverted pleats** With right sides together press the skirt panels toward the pleat inserts along the seamlines (**D** and **F**). Use a pin to mark the middle of each insert at its upper edge (**E**). Fold back the skirt panels on either side of the inserts so that the folds meet at **E**. Pin and tack the pleats at the upper edge. Press the pleats to the lower edge of the skirt.

6 **Assembling the table cloth** Stitch piping around the top panel, if desired, and attach the skirt following steps 6 and 7, *Making a Box-pleated Table Cloth*.

7 **Making the ties** Cut eight strips of fabric measuring 5 x 46cm (2 x 18in). With right sides together, fold each strip in half lengthways and stitch a 1cm (⅜in) seam along the long edge. Centre the seam and press it open. Turn right side out. Turn in the raw edges and slipstitch closed.

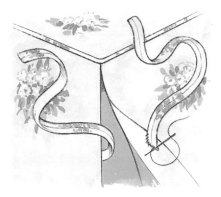

8 **Stitching the ties** At each skirt corner measure and pin 12.5cm (5in) down from the upper edge. Tuck the end of a tie behind each opening edge of the pleat at the marks. Taking care that the stitches don't show at the front, handstitch the ties in place.

DRESSING TABLE SKIRTS

Freshen up your bedroom with a romantic skirted dressing table. The skirt is both decorative and functional, disguising an old table and keeping stored items out of sight.

A covered dressing table makes a delightful addition to your bedroom. You can buy a dressing table base by mail order or from a shop and then make a cover to coordinate with your decor.

The cover can be as elaborate or simple as you want. Whatever the style, choose a light to mediumweight furnishing fabric, such as chintz, so that the cover doesn't look too bulky.

Traditionally, covered dressing tables are kidney shaped, but you could easily cover a rectangular or square table to serve the same purpose. The table itself does not need to be smart, as scuffs and scratches will no longer show. If your table has drawers or shelving underneath, the cover must have a front opening for access.

A cover made in coordinating checked and striped fabrics gives this kidney shaped dressing table a smart, up-to-date image.

MAKING A TWO-PIECE COVER

Kidney-shaped dressing tables with a track around the edge of the top need a two-piece cover: a skirt that hangs from the track, and a top with a frill or edging that covers it. If your dressing table has no track but you still want to make a two-piece cover, attach the skirt with gathering tape pushed against double-sided tape, or hang it on eyelets from screw eyes.

This skirt has a front opening which allows you to get to the dressing table drawers. If you don't need access, make the cover without the opening – the fullness of the skirt will still allow you to sit comfortably at the dressing table.

Although it is not essential, adding a lining as well as backing the top will neaten the seams and give it a padded finish.

See pages 11-12 for adding piping.

1 **Making a pattern for the top** Lay a sheet of paper on top of the table and press it around the sides to mark the edge. Cut the paper out, following the creases. Then check the fit on the table and adjust the shape as necessary.

3 **Cutting out the cover top** Pin the pattern for the top on the straight grain of the fabric. Centre any prominent design motif before you cut. Cut out, adding 1.5cm (⅝in) seam allowance all round.

4 **Cutting out the lining** Using the cover top as a pattern, cut out two lining pieces – one for a backing and the other as a lining – adding a 1.5cm (⅝in) seam allowance. With wrong sides together, tack one lining piece to the cover top. Treat this as one piece when stitching on the frill.

2 **Measuring up for the skirt** Measure round the top (**A**). Then measure the drop from the track to floor (**B**), adding 8cm (3¼in) for heading and hem. Cut sufficient lengths to this measurement, so that when joined selvedge to selvedge they make a piece 1½ times the measurement round the top for standard fabrics.

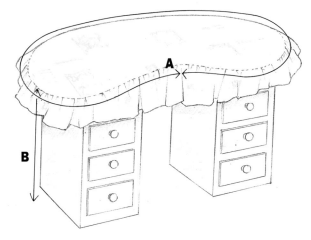

5 **Cutting the frill** Decide what depth you want the frill to be, adding 2cm (¾in) for hem and 1.5cm (⅝in) for seam allowances. Cut enough strips of fabric to this depth so that when joined end to end they make a piece 1½-2½ times the measurement round the top, depending on the type of fabric.

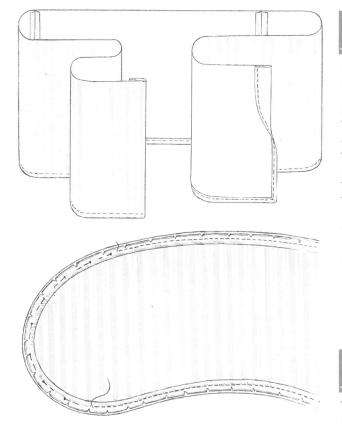

6 **Making the skirt** Pin then stitch the fabric pieces for the skirt together, selvedge to selvedge, to make one long piece. Press seams open. Turn under and pin a double 1.5cm (⅝in) side hem at each short end; machine stitch. Then turn and pin a double 1.5cm (⅝in) hem along the lower edge of the fabric. Stitch by hand or machine. To hide the skirt hems, fold under each centre front edge for 5cm (2in) and pin back.

7 **Adding heading tape** Turn 5cm (2in) to the wrong side along the top edge of the skirt and pin standard heading tape along the top. Stitch in place along the outer edges of the tape. Pull up the tape cords so the skirt fits the track, knot cords and hang skirt using curtain hooks, with the split at the front.

8 **Adding piping** Make up enough piping to go around the top cover plus 2.5cm (1in) overlap. With raw edges matching, position piping to the right side of cover top and tack. Snip into piping seams for ease around curves.

◀ *The smart red and white stripes of this two-piece dressing table cover make a pleasing contrast to the floral curtains and wallpaper. The stripes and frills of the cover are wittily echoed in the lamp bases.*

TIP

GLASS FINISH
Whatever the shape of your dressing table, it is a good idea to have a piece of glass cut to fit the top. It will keep your cover clean and anchor it in place. If buying a kit, check first – some come with a pre-cut piece of glass.

9 Stitching frill Join frill sections to give one continuous piece, pressing seams open. Pin and stitch a double 1cm (⅜in) hem on the lower edge. Machine or hand-stitch braid in place if using.

10 Gathering the frill Fold the frill in half and mark the centre points of the fabric on the top edge with two pins. Run two rows of gathering stitches along the top edge 1cm (⅜in) and 1.2cm (½in) from the raw edge, starting and stopping at the centre marks. On the cover top, mark the centre back with a pin. With right sides facing and matching marked points, pin the frill at the centre back. Pull up the gathering threads until the frill fits the cover top, then arrange the gathers evenly all the way round.

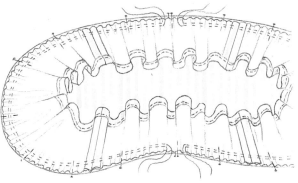

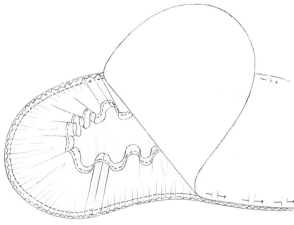

11 Attaching the frill Pin the gathered frill all the way round the top, right sides together, then tack and stitch in place, taking a 1.5cm (⅝in) seam. Remove tacking and gathering, and trim the seams at an angle to grade them.

12 Lining the top Fold up the frill on to the cover top and lay the second lining piece on top with right sides together. Pin around outer edges, taking care not to catch in the frill. Stitch following previous stitching line, leaving an opening at the back. Clip into curves and turn to right side through opening. Slipstitch opening closed. Press top and arrange it on the table with the frill covering the track.

GATHERED COVER

It is possible to turn a little table or inexpensive desk into an attractive dressing table in your bedroom by hiding it under a full skirted cover. This gathered cover is made in the same way as the top section of the two piece cover. Simply treat the skirt as an extra long frill which has an opening at the front.

The cord is stitched on by hand, after the cover is complete. Alternatively, you can leave the seam plain, or insert contrast piping into it before you stitch the skirt to the top.

YOU WILL NEED

❖ TABLE to cover

❖ PAPER for pattern

❖ FABRIC (see steps 1 and 2 for amounts)

❖ LINING – twice table top amount (see step 1)

❖ PINS, NEEDLES, SCISSORS, THREAD, TAPE MEASURE

❖ DECORATIVE CORD (optional)

▶ See page 108 for attaching cord.

1 **Cutting out the top** Make a pattern for the cover top as given in Step 1, *Making a Two-piece Cover*. Cut out one from fabric and two from lining, adding 1.5cm (⅝in) for seams. With wrong sides together, tack one lining piece to the cover top. Treat this as one piece when stitching on the skirt.

2 **Measuring up for the skirt** Measure and make up the skirt as in Steps 2 and 6, *Making a Two-piece Cover*. No heading allowance is needed, so only add 4.5cm (1¾in) for the hem and seam allowance to the length.

▲ *With a gathered cover, any old table, whether rectangular, round or square, can serve as a stylish dressing table. A glass top protects the fabric from spills.*

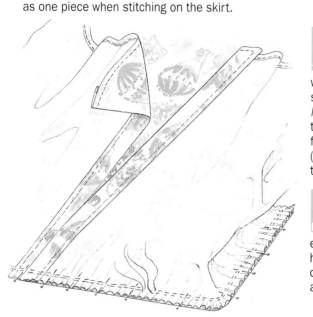

3 **Gathering the skirt** Fold the skirt in half, end to end, and mark the middle of the fabric at the top edge with a pin. Gather and fit the skirt in the same way as the frill in Steps 10 and 11, *Making a Two-piece Cover*, overlapping the short edges of the skirt slightly at the front. If adding cord, leave a small 2cm (¾in) opening at the centre back to hide the cord ends.

5 **Attaching cord** Cut enough cord to go around cover top, allowing a 1.2cm (½in) overlap. Push the cord ends into the seam opening, and handstitch cord in place. Then slipstitch opening in lining closed. Press top and arrange it over the table.

4 **Lining the cover top** Add the lining as for Step 12, *Making a Two-piece Cover*.

Decorative edgings

Trimmings add impact to your upholstery, curtains or lampshades.

The range of decorative edgings and trimmings available today is huge – you can find a trimming to enhance, outline, emphasize or harmonize with every conceivable colour, style and type of upholstery or furnishing on the market.

Selecting suitable trimmings

The weight and type of trim should be in keeping with the fabric and style of the item being trimmed. Put light trims on lightweight fabrics and reserve heavy trims for heavier fabrics that can support them. As a general rule, use shiny, elaborate trims on rich formal fabrics; on a simple fabric like cotton, use an appropriate cotton trim.

Also consider how the trim is to be attached – some, like flanged cord, should be attached when the main seams are stitched, others are fixed after making up to cover seams or tacks. Before you start, work out at what stage you need to apply the trimming.

Find out whether the trim is washable before you buy it – don't apply a dry-clean-only border to washable curtains unless you want to unpick it every time your drapes get grubby.

Types of trims

Braids (2) are tightly woven bands used as decorative borders on cushions, curtains and furniture to accentuate shape. They range in width from 6-150mm (¼-6in) and in style from plain ribbed bands to ornately patterned, embroidered strips with looped, or picot, edgings. Use colourful or ornate braids to add different textures and patterns to plain fabrics, or as a useful way to disguise joins in lengthened curtains.

Cords and ropes (4) are used like piping to emphasize the outline of chairs, cushions and window dressings. Heavy cords and ropes can be used as tiebacks. They come in every colour and texture from natural cotton and twisted paper to sumptuous gold thread and chenille. *Flanged cords* (5) have a taped edge that is stitched into a seam.

Fringes range from simple, single colour examples made from lightweight synthetic fibres to ornate, multi-coloured versions in a mixture of luxurious yarns. Natural fibre fringes in cotton, linen or silk can be dyed to match any colour scheme. *Bullion fringe* (7) is composed of rows of tightly twisted skeins which form the fringe attached to a heading; heavy luxurious versions are normally used as skirting for chairs and sofas.

Cut fringe has a cut edge and moves freely; lighter than bullion fringe, it can be used on all kinds of soft furnishings.

Block fringe is composed of two or more colours arranged in blocks and can be used to provide a dramatic edging to a plain fabric. *Scalloped and fanned fringes* have shaped edges.

Tasselled fringe (8) has rows of small tassels or tufts attached to a heading. *Bobble fringe* has miniature pompons, hung from a narrow braid heading. It is a traditional favourite for cushions, lampshades and as shelf edging.

Gimp or upholsterer's braid (6) is made of strands of silk-covered cord loosely woven into decorative bands. It is normally used to cover tacks on antique style furniture. The weave ensures that it can easily be laid round curved shapes, making it the ideal trim for scalloped pelmets.

Ribbons can be used in the same decorative ways as braid, but they are softer, so require different handling. Like braids, there is a huge range of ribbons from simple satins to rich brocades and velvet.

Ruche (3) is a fancy, three dimensional looped or fringed edging. It is especially popular for sofas and cushions and, like piping, is sewn into seams. For ease of working, some types have a loose line of stitching holding the outer edge firm – when it is in place, the loose stitching is removed so the surface fluffs up.

Tassels (1) range from small simple styles made in one yarn to elaborate, multi-tasselled versions in combinations of different yarns.

Working with trimmings

The way that you attach a trimming will depend on the type of trim, where you are adding it and how much wear and tear it will receive. Essentially there are four methods – stitching by hand or machine, glueing, fusing with an iron-on bonding web and using upholsterer's tacks. The last three no-sew methods will be dealt with as they occur in future soft furnishing projects.

Cutting the trim

Many trimmings will unravel when they are cut – and continue to unravel as you work with them. To avoid this happening, wrap clear sticky tape firmly around the cutting position and cut in the centre of the tape.

Alternatively, wind a strong thread tightly round the cut end, holding it firm with a dab of general purpose adhesive.

Pre-shrinking trims

When using a cotton or linen trim on items to be washed, you need to pre-shrink the trim before attaching it. Hold a steaming iron just above it, then press with right side down on a towel to prevent flattening. If it's washable, and will be attached to a washable fabric, soak in hot water briefly, dry on a towel and press as before.

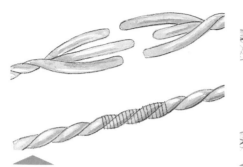

To join cord Unravel each cord end a short way. Trim the individual cords to different lengths, then twist them together. Dab with glue to secure, then bind the join with thread.

To join the flanged ends of two lengths of cord so that they form a continuous piece, unravel a short length and intertwine the strands. Stitch the intertwined ends to the fabric.

To neaten fringing fold under raw ends 6mm (¼in) and slipstitch down. To join two lengths, fold under raw ends and butt folded edges together. Slipstitch join closed and turnings flat.

Stitching cord

Cord is slipstitched in place by hand. Leave a small gap in the seam or unpick a small opening in a ready made item, and cut the cord about 5cm (2in) longer than you need. Tuck one end inside the gap, and fasten in place underneath. Then stitch the cord along the seam with small even stitches. Tuck the remaining end inside at the gap, neatly stitching the ends together. When adding cord to awkward and inflexible areas – such as an upholstered chair – use a curved upholsterer's needle.

Flanged cord Treat flanged cord like piping, inserting it into the seam and allowing ease for corners. To neaten ends, pull the cord into the seam. On continuous lengths, butt or slightly overlap the ends (see *Sewing Facts 1*) .

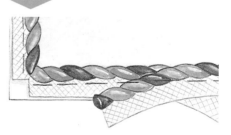

Stitching fringing

Topstitching Machine stitch the fringe over a narrow hem. Stitch close to the top and bottom edges of the heading.

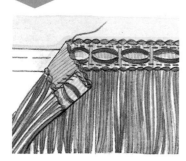

Hand stitch fringing on to ready made items when it is difficult to use a sewing machine. On upholstery, you may need to use a curved upholstery needle.

Inserting fringing Light fringing with a simple headings can be inserted into a seam. Position fringing on the main fabric right sides together, so the heading aligns with seam allowance. Trim to length, allowing 6mm (¼in) turnings each end. Fold ends back and tack fringe in place. Position lining, right side down on top. Machine stitch along edges of fringe heading.

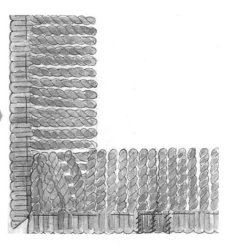

LAMPSHADE COVERS

Frilled, flounced and flirty, these lampshade covers will transform a plain shade into a romantic delight. The covers simply slip on top of an existing shade and can be made in any lightweight fabric.

Dressing up a plain lampshade with a flirty skirted cover gives it a new, frivolous image. Lightweight, crisp or sheer fabrics make ideal covers. Choose a colour that will bathe the room in a warm, flattering light – white, creams and pinks all create a pretty mood.

Use either an old shade or buy an inexpensive one. If the colour of the shade is wrong, make the skirt in an opaque fabric – taffeta, light silks or fine cotton are suitable. If you are happy with the colour of the shade, show it off with a sheer skirt that lets the base colour peek through.

A dotted voile shade cover, trimmed with green ribbon and a silk flower to match its surroundings, prettily disguises an old, shaped lampshade underneath.

SHAPED SHADES

This method covers a shaped shade with a lining petticoat, then a separate gathered skirt; both are held in place with elastic casings. The lining fits over the the base and upper edges of the shade, while the skirt sits partway down on top, with the join hidden by a wide ribbon. Make good use of trimmings – edge the skirt in a silky ribbon or lightweight braid and draw the eye to the waist of the shade with a jaunty bow, rosettes or a single silk bloom.

▶ See pages 31-32 for details of basic seams.

1 Measuring shade Measure round the base of the shade (**A**) with a tape measure, and add 4cm (1½in) for seam. Measure down one side (**B**) and add 8cm (3¼in) to make casings for the elastic. Decide on the depth of the skirt (**C**) and add 1.5cm (⅝in) for the hem. Take a note of the measurements.

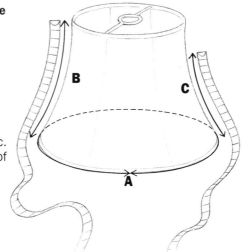

2 Calculating fabric amounts Using measurements plus seam allowances from step 1, draw one rectangle **A** x **B** on newspaper with a pencil and ruler. Draw a second rectangle **C** x twice the length of **A**, to give the fullness allowance for gathering. You need to cut out one of each of these rectangles in fabric; use the paper patterns to estimate fabric amounts.

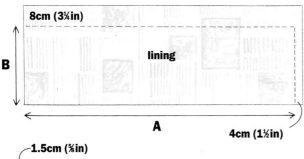

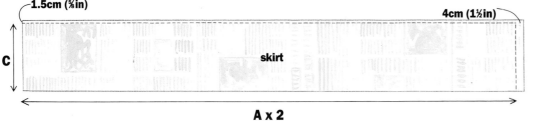

3 Cutting out Pin the paper patterns to the fabric and cut out one lining and one skirt rectangle on the straight grain.

4 Stitching the lining and skirt Using a French seam, join the short ends of the lining. On both long raw edges, turn up a 3mm (⅛in) then a 12mm (½in) double hem as a casing for the elastic. Machine stitch hems, leaving a small opening in each to insert elastic.

Again using a French seam, stitch short ends of skirt together. Turn up a 3mm (⅛in) hem along one long edge and machine stitch; then turn up the hem by another 3mm (⅛in) and machine stitch.

5 Fitting the lining Thread the elastic through each casing and hold ends together with safety pins. Put lining over shade, pulling up the elastic to fit snugly round base and top. Trim ends and stitch together. Slip stitch openings closed.

◁ *Gathered lampshade skirts can be made to fit most shapes of shade: the pink taffeta skirt hides a bowed drum shade, while the flocked sheer skirt tops a plain white coolie shade – instructions for this are given overleaf.*

8 To finish Slip the skirt on to the lining that is already fitted over the shade. Tie a coordinating ribbon round the waist of the skirt to conceal the join, holding it in place with a few hand stitches. Trim the shade with a separate bow, rosette or fabric flower.

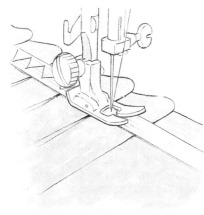

6 Measuring the skirt elastic Hold the elastic round the shade where the top of the skirt is to sit; it should be slightly stretched to hug the shade gently. Trim elastic and stitch ends together to form a ring.

7 Attaching elastic Fold the elastic ring into quarters and mark the folds with pins. Then fold the skirt into quarters and mark these folds with pins too. With the two sets of pins matching, pin the elastic to the wrong side of the raw top edge of the skirt. Stretching elastic and pleating skirt as you sew, machine zigzag stitch elastic to skirt fabric.

▶ *A mint green ribbon trim serves a dual purpose on this dotted voile shade – it hides the top of the separate skirt and binds the hem for a neat finish.*

COOLIE SHADE

Conical coolie shades can also be fitted with frilly skirts. Instructions for making the daisy patterned sheer cover on the previous page are given here. This skirt is simply glued to the top of a small, white coolie shade. Standard coolie shades are readily available and quite inexpensive. If you don't have an old shade that needs covering, buy one specially in a suitable colour.

YOU WILL NEED

❖ COOLIE LAMPSHADE
❖ TAPE MEASURE, RULER, PENCIL and SCISSORS
❖ NEWSPAPER
❖ FABRIC (see step 1 for amount)
❖ MATCHING SEWING THREAD
❖ 35mm (1⅜in) wide RIBBON for binding top edge and bow
❖ ALL PURPOSE ADHESIVE

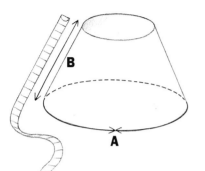

1 **Measuring shade** Measure round the base of the shade (**A**) and add 4cm (1½in) for seam. Measure down side (**B**) and add 6mm (¼in). Using a pencil and ruler, draw a rectangle twice the length of **A** x **B**, plus seams, on newspaper, and work out fabric amounts.

2 **Cutting out** Using the pattern, cut out a rectangle of fabric on the straight grain. Using a French seam, join the short ends of the rectangle together.

coolie shade skirt

6mm (¼in)   4cm (1½in)

B

A x 2

Tulle or stiff net makes an extra quick lampshade cover, as it doesn't need hemming. Since the shade will show through, choose a colour that works with your decor. Make up as for the coolie shade, allowing for a small frill at the top. Hide gathering with a ribbon bow or cluster of rose buds.

3 **Neatening the hem** Turn up a 3mm (⅛in) hem on one long edge, and machine stitch. Turn up the hem again by 3mm (⅛in) and machine stitch.

T I P

TULLE SKIRTS

Give very fine or floppy fabrics body with a stiff net petticoat, so that they stand out crisply from the base of the shade. Measure up one side of the shade, across the top and down the other side and cut out a circle of net to this diameter. Drape the net circle symmetrically over the shade and cut away the disc shape of net covering the top. Make up the skirt as described, tacking the net in place before binding the top edge.

4 **Gathering the top edge** Fold skirt into quarters and mark folds with pins. Stitch two rows of gathering round top edge, stopping and starting at pins. Then divide top of shade into quarters, and mark positions lightly with pencil. Slip cover over shade and, matching pins to quarter marks, draw up gathering threads to fit round top. Even out gathering, tie threads to secure and slip cover off again.

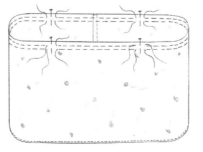

5 **Binding top edge** Cut a piece of ribbon to fit top of shade, plus 1.5cm (⅝in) overlap. Fold ribbon to cover gathered edge of skirt, turning in one raw end, and tack in place. Machine stitch close to edge of ribbon, catching down both sides and holding the gathers at the same time.

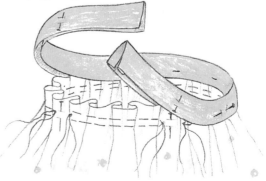

6 **To finish** Place the skirt on the shade and hold in place with a few dabs of all purpose adhesive. Hide the join in the ribbon binding with a bow made from the remainder of the ribbon.

Making your own fabric or paper lampshade is not difficult and a good way of cutting costs.

Whether on table lamps or pendant lights, lampshades are key items of soft furnishing in a room. Not only are they essential sources of artificial light, but also important linking elements in the design scheme. Making your own shade is a good way of matching it to the layout and saving money at the same time.

Lampshade equipment

On the right is a useful guide to the most popular lampshade shapes available. You can buy new frames for most of these shapes from craft suppliers. However, if you have difficulty in tracking down any of the more unusual frames, junk shops and car boot or garage sales are often good places to find an interesting old shade that you can re-cover to suit your taste.

Frames

A frame consists of an upper and a lower ring held apart by struts, and is the base for the shade. These rings and the shaping of the struts determine the distinctive style of each lampshade.

In a *drum frame*, for example, the upper and lower rings have the same diameter. They are joined by straight, vertical struts to make a cylindrical shape. In an elegant *bowed empire frame*, on the other hand, the upper ring is smaller than the lower one and the struts gently curve inwards

Fittings

Each frame also has a means of attaching it to the light fitting. On a table lamp, the lampshade is often fitted to the lamp base via the ring and pivoted struts of a gimbal fitting, or it is balanced on a separate shade support attached to the light fitting. Small candlelamp shades usually have bulb clips that simply fit round the bulb to support the shade. Ceiling lampshades hang from pendant fittings at the top of the shade.

Materials

You need the following items for preparing and covering a frame:
Binding tape is a strong, woven cotton tape used to bind a frame so a shade can be stitched to it.
Self-adhesive paper tape is used to bind the frame of a non-sewn shade.
Enamel paint is used to seal the bare metal of the frame.

Parchment in a rigid sheet is used for a smooth-sided lampshade.
Self-adhesive PVC/plastic (Stik It) is a rigid PVC sheet with a self-adhesive surface on to which fabric or other material is stuck.
Trimmings are sewn or glued round the edges of a shade for decorative effect and to neaten it.

Fabric

Consider the following points when choosing fabric for a shade:
❖ Check the way the fabric transmits light by holding it up to a direct light.
❖ For an unlined shade use a mediumweight, closely woven fabric to ensure the light fittings are not visible through the shade.
❖ Line the shade or back it with a lightweight interfacing if the light fittings are visible.
❖ The colour of the fabric tints the light cast by the lamp. For a cool light use blue and green shades; reds and

yellows create a warmer glow.
❖ Heavyweight and dark fabrics throw the light to top and bottom of the shade, creating directional lighting.
❖ For pleated shades, avoid thick fabrics that are difficult to pleat. If the sides of the shade slope the pattern becomes more visible at the base. Pleat up some fabric to see how it looks.
❖ Fitted shades require a soft fabric and lining with stretch across the bias. Also check that the print or weave of the fabric looks good on the diagonal.

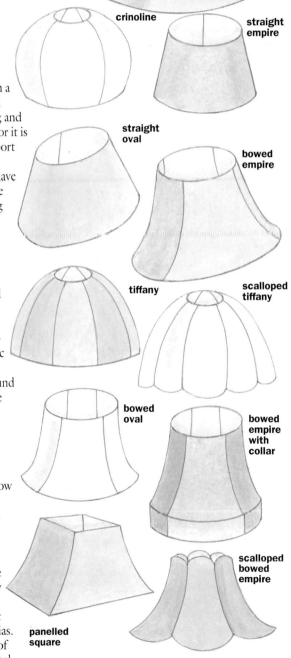

drum
bowed drum
coolie
crinoline
straight empire
straight oval
bowed empire
tiffany
scalloped tiffany
bowed oval
bowed empire with collar
panelled square
scalloped bowed empire

Preparing a lampshade frame

When you are covering a lampshade frame you may need to do some preparatory work on the frame first. This depends on the type of frame and the cover you are making. For example, if you're making a simple card cover for a plastic coated frame, no preparation is necessary, as you can glue the card directly on to the frame. However, if the frame is made of plain metal, you need to paint it with white enamel paint to prevent rust. If you are using an old frame, it may already show some signs of rust. In this case, sand the frame down before painting it. If you are going to sew the lampshade cover to the frame, you need to paint the frame and then wind tape round it before starting to fix the fabric to the frame.

Painting a frame

If the metal frame is not PVC/plastic coated it is important, for a fabric or a paper shade, to paint it before covering.

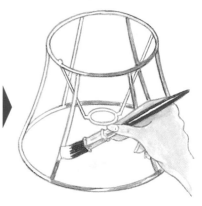

Remove any rust by rubbing it with sandpaper. File off any rough or sharp areas that might snag the fabric of the shade cover. Paint the frame struts and rings with white enamel paint but do not paint the gimbal – the central ring that fits round the light bulb holder.

Taping a frame

If you are making a sewn fabric lampshade you need to bind the frame with cotton tape to provide a foundation for the stitches. Do not bind the gimbal or pendant light fittings. Estimate the amount of tape required by measuring the length of the frame struts and rings, and multiplying the total by three. If white tape shows through under a dark fabric, dye the tape with cotton fabric dye to match the shade.

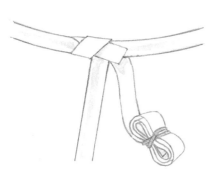

1 Taping the first strut Cut a piece of tape three times the length of one strut. Holding one end of the tape on the outside top end of the strut, take the tape length over the top ring, then wind it round the strut to secure the loose end. Pulling the tape very tightly, wrap it diagonally down the strut, so that each turn just covers and secures the previous one. Once the binding is complete, the tape should not move.

2 Securing the strut tape At the bottom of the strut, take the tape over the bottom ring and back through the last tape loop to form a knot. Pull the tape tightly and leave the loose end free. Bind all but one of the remaining struts in the same way.

3 Taping the top ring Measure round the top and bottom rings and the untaped strut. Cut tape three times this length. Wind up the tape and secure it with an elastic band, leaving 20cm (8in) free. Hold the free end of tape on the outside of the top ring, at the top of untaped strut. Wrap the tape length over and round the top ring and over the loose end to secure it.

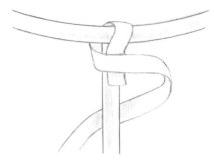

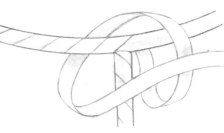

4 Completing the taping Bind the tape round the top ring, wrapping in a figure of eight at each strut. When you reach the untaped strut, wrap a figure of eight then work down the strut. At the bottom end, wrap a figure of eight and work round the bottom ring. At each strut cut the loose tape end to 1cm (⅜in) and cover it with a figure of eight wound over it. At the end, trim the tape to 6mm (¼in), turn under and hand stitch the raw edge in place.

Choosing bases

It is important to check that the base and shade work well together and that the two are appropriately proportioned. If possible take the lampshade base with you when you are choosing the shade or vice versa. There are a few general guidelines that you should bear in mind when you are matching lampshades and bases.

❖ The shade should be deep enough to cover the fitting but not so deep that it obscures the base.
❖ The lower edge of the shade should be twice the width of the base at its widest point.
❖ For a round or vase shaped base the shade should be one to two times the height of the base
❖ The shade of a column or candlestick base should be one-third the height of base.

FABRIC ROSES

Fabric roses, sewn by hand or machine, add a fresh and individual look to soft furnishings, and are inexpensive to make made from scraps of pretty fabric.

R esembling extravagant, old-fashioned cabbage roses, these fabric roses look professional, yet are very easy to make, even for those with limited sewing experience. The rose petals are formed from different sized triangles of fabric, layered together and stitched by hand. It's a method that guarantees good results.

You can use almost any fabric, depending on the look you want to achieve, although it is best to avoid heavy or very stiff fabrics, such as canvas, which are difficult to shape and hard to stitch. For a rich, plush look make the roses in velvet, choosing deep, realistic rose colours such as crimson, red or luminous pink. In filmy muslins, the resulting rose is much more delicate, while made in natural cottons they'll be understated. In bright, clear colours they add a splash of informal fun to a room.

Apply roses singly or in clusters to trim all sorts of items, from cushions, fabric-covered photograph frames or covered storage boxes to the edge of a table cloth or a hat you want to display on a wall – or even wear! Roses trimming the edge of a tieback or the base of goblet pleats on a curtain look charming; or scatter them all over a bedspread for a fairy-tale touch in a girl's room.

Cabbage roses are easily sewn by hand and stitched to a ready-made cushion to give a completely individual look that allows you to link new fabrics with existing furnishings.

MAKING FABRIC ROSES

The roses are based on squares of fabric, folded across the bias into triangles. Four triangles are stitched together to form a square and this becomes one petal layer – the roses shown were made with three petal layers and a separate centre. You can make the roses to any size by changing the size of the squares. For small roses

it is a good idea to use a lightweight fabric which is easily twisted. For medium-sized roses in thicker fabrics, you may find you need only two petal layers. This is an economical method – you should be able to make several roses from a 50cm (20in) length of fabric. Neaten the back of each rose with a small fabric circle.

1 Cutting outer petals Cut out four 12.5cm (5in) squares, on the straight grain. Wrong sides together, fold each square in half diagonally and press. Along the folded edge, press a further 6mm (¼in) to the back. Open out the narrow fold.

2 Positioning triangles Lay triangle **A** flat, with the back uppermost, and pin triangle **B** on top so the folded edges intersect at right angles and the raw edges are even. Overlap and pin remaining triangles **C** and **D** in the same way to form a square. Lift up **A** to tuck corner of last triangle to back.

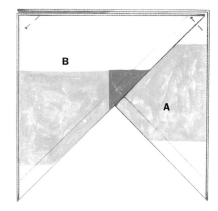

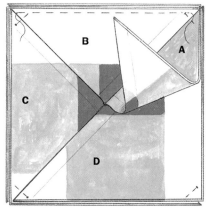

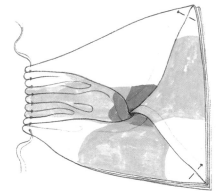

3 Gathering petal layers Using double thread, sew large gathering stitches along one side of the square. Pull up the gathering tightly and secure with backstitches. Repeat along the remaining sides of the square so the folded edges turn to the outside, to form one layer of petals. Finger press narrow folds to the back.

4 Making petal layers Make up a second and third layer of petals following steps 1 to 3, this time using 10cm (4in) and 7.5cm (3in) fabric squares respectively.

5 Making rose centre Cut 12.5 x 5cm (5 x 2in) fabric strip on bias. Fold in half lengthways and press. Along folded edge, press a further 6mm (¼in) to the back. Open out narrow fold. Sew gathering stitches along raw edges, curving towards folded edge at ends. Cut corners into a curve. Pull up stitches until strip is half the original length. Wrap strip around itself and press narrow fold to outside. Stitch securely at base.

6 Arranging petal layers Place the centre of the rose inside the smallest petal layer and handstitch securely together so stitches are not visible from the top of rose. Arrange the larger petal layers around them, stitching layers together one at a time.

7 Neatening rose Cut a circle of fabric 6.5cm (2½in) in diameter. Using slipstitch, handstitch the circle to the back of the rose, tucking raw edges under as you work. Stitch the roses in place on the cushion or other soft furnishings.

A TAILORED BOW

Just as a shiny ribbon bow makes a gift-wrapped present look special, the addition of a fabric bow gives an extra flourish to your decorating scheme.

Attached to the skirt of an occasional table or to a ticback, or hung on the wall behind a picture, an ornamental fabric bow with long flaring tails adds a charming extravagance to a room. You can also coordinate accessories like cushion covers with other soft furnishings in the room by making a decorative bow from curtain or upholstery fabric.

The choice of fabric and the bow's proportions are crucial to making a successful bow. Use a soft fabric for big floppy bows – silk dupion looks and feels luxurious and is easy to work. Lightweight satin, chintz and soft cottons are also good choices. For picture bows use a stiffer fabric, or line a flimsy fabric with stiffening net. To determine the best proportions for your bow when it's in position, make a test sample in calico or curtain lining.

The bow featured here is simply made from four rectangles of fabric – a bow section with two separate tails and a central loop instead of a knot – which are easy to run up on a sewing machine or stitch by hand. The furnishing cotton is interlined with net to give it extra body.

Four bows hold an attractively ruched net overskirt in place over a tablecloth in a toning fabric. Attached with Velcro, the bows can be put on and taken off when you want.

MAKING THE BOW

The measurements given here make a bow 20cm (8in) wide, with tails 28cm (11in) long. You can easily adjust the proportions to make a bigger bow or longer tails. A 1cm (⅜in) seam allowance has been included on all measurements.

1 **Cutting out** From the main fabric, cut one rectangle 22 x 28cm (8¾ x 11in) for the bow, then cut two rectangles 30 x 15cm (12 x 6in) for the tails and one square 10 x 10cm (4 x 4in) for the knot. With a striped fabric, make sure to line up the stripes in the right direction before cutting out the pieces.

2 **Making the bow** Place the net on to the wrong side of the fabric and tack all round, close to the edge. Fold the bow fabric widthways, right sides together, and sew along the long edges, leaving a 10cm (4in) opening in the centre for the zip. Press the seam open along the centre back of the bow. Sew across the short ends. Turn right side out through central opening, easing the corners out, and press. Slip stitch the opening closed.

3 **Making the tails** Fold one tail lengthways, right sides together and stitch long edges. Press seam open so it is centred on the back of the tail. Using a ruler and chalk, mark a 'V' in the end of the tail, with the point of the 'V' on the seam. Stitch 'V', trim along seam, clipping into centre and across corners. Turn to right side and press. Repeat for second tail.

4 **Making the knot** Fold the knot fabric widthways with right sides facing and sew the long raw edges. Press seam open. Turn to the right side, centring the seam on the back of the knot, and press.

5 **Gathering the bow** Run two rows of gathering stitches across the centre of the bow and pull threads up until 4cm (1½in) wide in the middle. Secure the gathering threads.

6 **Adding the knot** Wrap the knot strip round the centre of the bow to cover the gathers. Fold the raw edges in at the back and oversew to secure. Work a few stitches into the bow along the edge of the knot to hold it firmly in place.

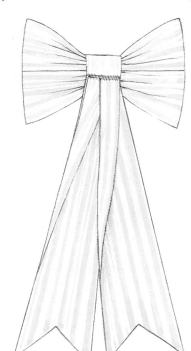

TIP

A DETACHABLE BOW

Cut a rectangle of Velcro Sew 'n Stick. Position the self-adhesive side on the wall, or whatever is being decorated. Stitch the sewing half to the back of the tails at knot height and press the bow in place. It can easily be removed again whenever you want a change.

7 **Adding the tails** Pleat the open end of each tail lengthways to make it 4cm (1½in) wide, and tack to secure. Arrange the ends so that one partially covers the other, with the tails slightly splayed. Pin them in place, squarely over the knot at the back of the bow, and sew in place.

▷ *A symmetrical fabric bow with elongated tails is a neat and simple way of turning even a small picture into a significant feature of the room.*

PADDED FRAMES

*Photographs displayed in fabric-covered frames,
made to suit any mood or theme, create a welcoming
and personal focal point to a room.*

F abric-covered photograph frames are attractive accessories for your home or a handsome gift to accompany a family portrait. They are easily made by covering frame mounts that you can buy from art shops or picture framers – frame mounts with oval apertures are ideal for portrait photographs. For even quicker results, use a photograph frame kit in which all the card pieces are already cut.

No sewing is involved. To pad the front, wadding is simply glued to the frame. Then the entire frame and stand are neatly covered in plain or printed fabric, which is also held in place with adhesive. You can either buy a special piece of fabric, or use a favourite remnant.

For an added personal touch, you can decorate the frame with a pattern of roses using simple embroidery stitches.

Padded photograph frames are economical to make using remnants of fabric and inexpensive cardboard mounts. With a unique handmade quality they're a good way to display treasured family photographs.

MAKING A PADDED PHOTOGRAPH FRAME

As a rough guide to fabric amounts, you need about four times the size of the frame plus 2cm (¾in) turnings all round. Choose closely woven, mediumweight fabrics. Avoid bulky fabrics that do not fold easily or slippery fabrics that are difficult to handle.

Use strong card for the frame back and stand. For an accurate, neat line cut the card with a sharp craft knife against a metal ruler. You can buy clear acrylic sheet in artists' supply shops.

1 Cutting the frame back Measure the length and width of the frame mount and, using a craft knife and metal rule, cut a piece of card this size less 3mm (⅛in) all round.

2 Cutting the fabric Cut two rectangles of fabric to the dimensions of the frame mount, plus 2cm (¾in) all round for turnings. Ensure patterned fabrics are well positioned on mount.

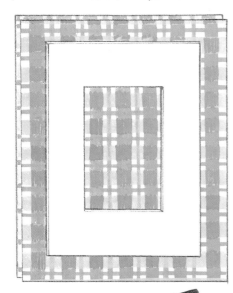

3 Cutting the wadding Apply spray adhesive to one side of the frame mount and lay it face down on the wadding. Using scissors, cut wadding from around the outside and inside of the frame.

4 Covering mount Apply spray adhesive to the wadded side of mount and lay it face down, centrally, on the wrong side of one of the rectangles of fabric. Cut away corners of fabric turnings to within 3mm (⅛in) of the corners of the card.

5 Gluing the turnings Spread PVA adhesive along one long turning and fold over to the wrong side of the frame. Without displacing card or wadding, pull fabric tight to the frame edge and press down firmly. Repeat on the other long edge. Glue one short edge, fold under narrow hems at the cut diagonal corners, fold over and stick to the wrong side of the frame. Repeat on the second short edge.

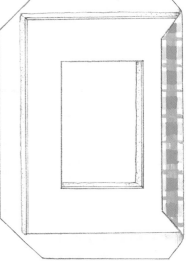

TIP

WEIGHTING DOWN
To make the fabric lie flat and reduce the fabric thickness at the corners, weight the frame pieces after gluing the fabric to each section. Lay the pieces carefully between two squares of wadding and press under a pile of books.

Make a selection of frames in a range of sizes and different patterned fabrics to display a group of photographs.

6 Gluing around frame aperture
Leaving a turning allowance of 2cm (¾in) all round, cut fabric from the centre of the frame. Make diagonal snips into the corners of fabric turnings to avoid bulk, stopping 2mm (¹⁄₁₆in) away from the card. Working on one edge at a time, spread PVA adhesive along turnings and fold through aperture. Pull the fabric tight to the frame edges and press down firmly on the back.

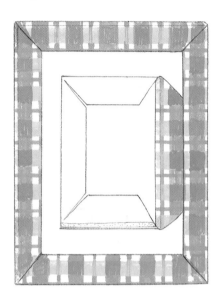

7 Covering outside of frame back
Apply spray adhesive to one side of the frame back and lay it face down, centrally, on the wrong side of the remaining piece of fabric. Glue turnings following step 5.

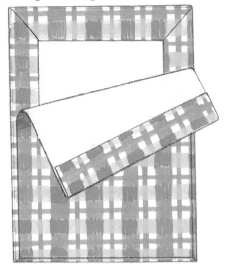

8 Neatening inside of frame back
Measure the length and width of the covered back and cut a piece of fabric this size, plus a 2cm (¾in) hem on one short side, and less 3mm (⅛in) on the other three sides. Turn under and glue the hem. Spread PVA on the wrong side of the fabric, and stick centrally on the frame back.

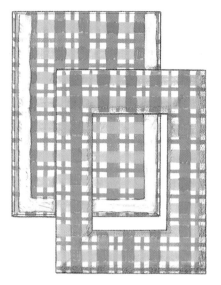

9 Assembling the frame
Spread PVA adhesive evenly along unhemmed short edge and both long edges of the inside frame back. Matching the hemmed edge of the frame back to the unglued edge of the frame front, stick front and back together. The unglued edge becomes the top of the frame. Cut a piece of clear acrylic sheet the size of the picture and slide into the frame through top opening.

MAKING THE STAND

1 Cutting out the stand
Cut a piece of card the shape of the diagram, so the long axis (**A**) measures 1cm (⅜in) less than the frame length. Score a fold along the dotted line. Cut a second piece of card the shape of the hatched area in the diagram.

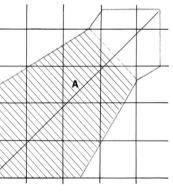

2 Cutting fabric for stand Using the card pieces as templates, cut two pieces of fabric to the same shapes, adding 2cm (¾in) all round for turnings.

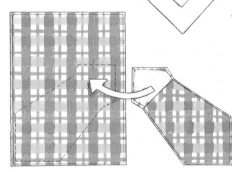

3 Covering the stand
Apply spray adhesive to card pieces and stick face down, centrally, on the wrong side of fabric pieces. Cut the turnings at each corner for ease. Using PVA, stick turnings to wrong sides of cards one at a time.

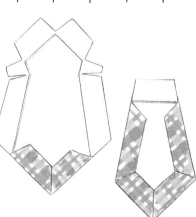

4 Completing the stand Spread PVA on wrong side of smaller stand piece. Matching edges, and with wrong sides facing, stick stand pieces together. Spread PVA on uncovered area of stand back. Matching lower left corner of frame and lower corner edges of stand, stick stand to back of frame.

MAKING AN EMBROIDERED OVAL FRAME

Frame mounts with oval apertures make perfect frames for portrait photographs. To ease the fabric round the curve of the aperture, clip into the turning allowance at regular intervals. Here the frame has been decorated with a pattern of roses and leaves worked in bullion knots. Stitch the embroidery design on the fabric before gluing it to the frame. As well as the materials on the previous page you need tailors' chalk, a needle and three colours of stranded embroidery cotton (see pages 23-24).

1 Preparing frame pieces
Follow steps 1-3 of *Padded Frame*. As a guide for placing the embroidered roses, use tailors' chalk to trace the edges of the frame on the right side of the piece of fabric cut for the front.

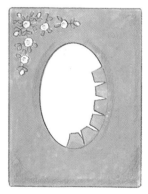

3 Working the leaves Using green embroidery cotton work a few leaves around the roses in bullion knots.

2 Working the roses Work the roses in bullion knots. Make two or three stitches in yellow alongside each other. Work longer, white knots in circles around them. For the buds, make one yellow and one or two white knots on either side.

A pattern of white roses and green leaves, embroidered in bullion knots, is worked on to the fabric before covering the frame front.

4 Covering the frame front
Follow steps 4-6 of *Padded Frame* to cover the frame front. Trim round the aperture, making snips approximately 1cm (³⁄₈in) apart to within 2mm (¹⁄₁₆in) of the card, all round the aperture turnings. Glue and stick a few tabs of fabric at a time to the wrong side.

5 Completing the frame Follow the remaining steps for *Padded Frame* in order to complete the frame and stand.

FABRIC-COVERED BOXES

*Store treasured keepsakes or odds and ends in an attractive
stack of no-sew fabric-covered boxes, simply made and ornamented with fine
ribbons, tassels and beads.*

Old cardboard boxes provide valuable extra storage space, but are often hidden away in cupboards or under beds. Covering them with fabric can simply and quickly transform plain boxes into decorative and practical containers that are good enough to display. Use a sturdy cardboard box with a lid,

such as an old shoe or hat box, and fabric in colours and patterns to tie in with the style of the room where you keep the box.

For a standard size shoe box you need approximately 1m (1⅛yd) of fabric. To create a softer, rounded shape, stick a thin layer of wadding to the lid of the box to pad it before covering.

Bring storage boxes out of the cupboard – when covered in a furnishing fabric, and trimmed artistically with bows or tassels, they make pretty storage accessories that are worth displaying.

COVERING AN OBLONG BOX

Choose firmly woven, mediumweight fabrics, avoiding fine or slippery fabrics as these are difficult to handle. To hold the fabric in place on outer surfaces use a light adhesive such as glue stick or spray adhesive. Secure turnings and edges with a stronger, general-purpose craft adhesive. To ensure that the adhesive does not mark the fabric test it on a piece of scrap fabric, allowing it time to dry.

YOU WILL NEED

❖ OBLONG BOX WITH LID
❖ FABRIC (see steps 1 and 5 for amount)
❖ TAPE MEASURE
❖ SCISSORS
❖ GLUE STICK or SPRAY ADHESIVE
❖ GENERAL PURPOSE CRAFT ADHESIVE
❖ TRIMMINGS (optional)

1 **Cutting fabric** Measure the depth (**A**) and around the outside of the box (**B**). Cut fabric to these measurements, adding 2.5cm (1in) to outer edge for turnings. Measure the dimensions of the box base (**C** x **D**) and cut a piece of fabric 1cm (⅜in) smaller all round.

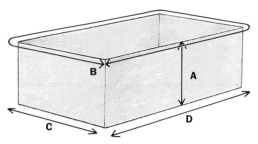

2 **Covering sides** Spread glue stick or spray adhesive thinly on one long side of the box. Smooth fabric along glued side of the box leaving a 2.5cm (1in) overlap on one short and both long edges. Work round the box, gluing one side at a time. When the overlap is reached press under remaining fabric so it is flush with the box edge and secure with general purpose craft adhesive.

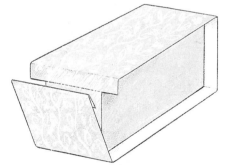

3 **Sticking on the base** Using craft adhesive, stick down the flaps of fabric on the short sides of the base, and then on the long sides, folding the corners on the diagonal. Spread craft adhesive on the base of the box and stick the base piece of fabric centrally in place.

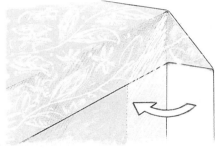

4 **Neatening top edge** Fold turnings to the inside and stick in place, tucking in extra fabric at corners. If the fabric is bulky, snip into the corners.

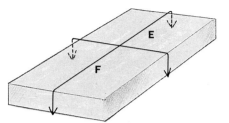

5 **Covering lid** Measure the lid both ways, including sides. Cut fabric to these dimensions (**E** x **F**), adding 2.5cm (1in) all round. Spread stick or spray adhesive on lid and place fabric centrally. Stick fabric to short, then long sides, tucking in extra at the corners. Fold and stick flaps of fabric inside lid.

6 **Lining box** (optional) For a neater finish, line the box with pieces of fabric-covered card made to fit the inside walls and base. The lining can be padded with a layer of wadding.

◁ *Hunt for odd pieces of braid and ribbon, or long-saved beads, buttons and tassels to trim your box.*

ROUND BOXES

Follow steps for the Oblong Box. On curved edges snip turnings before sticking. For lid, cut fabric larger than the top, glue in place, taking turnings to lid side. Neaten lid edge with braid or an extra strip of fabric (raw edges pressed under).

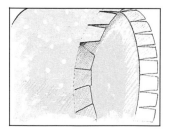

DRAWSTRING STORAGE

Humble drawstring bags have endless practical and decorative potential. Make them in coordinating fabrics – or use up remnants – and use them to store all sorts of homeless household items.

From outsized bags used for laundry to mini bags for pot-pourri, the method for making a basic drawstring bag is the same. Essentially, the bag consists of two rectangles of fabric joined at the sides and base, with a double hem at the open end that forms a casing. Two ties, threaded through the casing, draw the top of the bag closed and act as hangers.

Even a novice at a sewing machine can tackle making a drawstring bag with confidence. Made in an attractive fabric, a drawstring bag will add charm to a room and provide useful storage for anything from shoes and pot pourri to underwear.

Drawstring bags can be hung from any available object – the end of a bedstead, a curtain pole or even a door knob. A single decorative hook, or several hooks fixed under a shelf, offer a formal way of hanging one or a couple of bags. Alternatively to increase the storage capacity, you can put up a separate peg rail in a hallway or bedroom and hang several bags.

Modest drawstring bags hanging together on a peg rail become desirable storage accessories, especially when made up in a mix and match of lively fabrics.

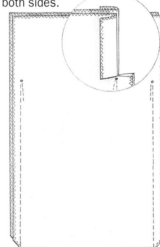

▲ *Mini-check and floral patterns create a charming collection of drawstring bags which is totally in keeping with the flowery country-style setting.*

Instead of making a conventional casing for the cords at the top of a drawstring bag, you can just sew a simple bag and bunch up the fabric around the neck, securing it with a wide, contrasting tie, or a length of ribbon, rope or cord.

YOU WILL NEED

❖ **70cm (¾yd) FABRIC** for a bag measuring 46 x 36cm (18 x 14in)
❖ **FABRIC PEN**
❖ **SEWING THREAD** to match fabric
❖ **1.6m (1¾yd) CORD**
❖ **BODKIN or large SAFETY PIN**

Choose a firm, sturdy cotton or cotton blend for making bags which will be used to hold bulky or weighty items. Furnishing weight chintz or cambric would be ideal. Light cottons, such as lawn, could be used to hold lingerie or other lightweight items. The tie can be made from a strip of self fabric, cord, ribbon, string or fine rope.

1 Cutting out Fold fabric in half with selvedges together, and cut two rectangles 64 x 34cm (25¼ x 13¼in). This allows 1.5cm (⅝in) seam allowances on the base and both sides, and for a 15cm (6in) turn over and casing at the top. On wrong side of fabric, make fabric pen marks on the seam line 16cm (6¼in) down from the top on both sides.

2 Sewing the bag Pin, tack and stitch bag round sides and base, going from mark to mark. Backstitch at marks to lock. Trim across corners. To neaten all seams, turn under 6mm (¼in) and stitch, or use zigzag.

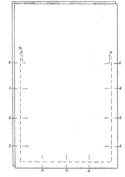

3 Preparing for the casing Using sharp scissors, carefully snip into the seam allowances at the marks on both sides, taking care not to cut into the stitching. Above marks, press seam allowances open.

4 Stitching the casing On wrong side of bag, fold casing allowances back to marks on both sides. Tuck under raw edges, pin and tack. Work one row of stitches close to raw edge, another 2.5cm (1in) above.

5 Adding the drawstrings Cut cord into two equal lengths. Using a bodkin or safety pin, thread each cord round the bag through front and back casings and pull the cords out on opposite sides. Finish each cord by knotting or with a neat seam.

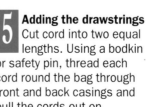

Index

ACKNOWLEDGEMENTS

Photographs

7 Rectella, 9 IPC Magazines/Robert Harding Syndication, 10 Ametex, 11, 12 Eaglemoss Publications/Martin Chaffer, 13 Eaglemoss Publications/Graham Rae, 19, 20 Eaglemoss Publications/Simon Page-Ritchie, 21, 22 Eaglemoss Publications/Graham Rae, 23, 24 Eaglemoss Publications/Jonathon Pollock, 25, 27 Ariadne Holland, 28 Sanderson, 29, 30 Eaglemoss Publications/Simon Page-Ritchie, 33 IPC Magazines/Robert Harding Syndication, 34 Eaglemoss Publications/Simon Page-Ritchie, 35 Biggie Best, 36 EWA/Rodney Hyett, 37 Eaglemoss Publications/Simon Page-Ritchie, 39 EWA/Dennis Stone, 40 Integra, 41 Dorma, 42 Rufflette, 43 Eaglemoss Publications/Steve Tanner, 45, 46(t) Kaleidoscope, 46(c,b) Eaglemoss Publications/Mark Wood, 47 Houses & Interiors, 48, 49 Pavilion Textiles, 50(tl) Laura Ashley Home, 50(tr) Doehet Zelf, 50(b) EWA/Mark Luscombe-Whyte, 51 Shand Kydd, 53, 54 IPC Magazines/Robert Harding Syndication, 55 Sanderson, 56 EWA/Neil Lorimer, 57, 58 IPC Magazines/Robert Harding Syndication, 59, 60 Romo Ltd, 61 Sanderson, 63, 64 Eaglemoss Publications/Martin Chaffer, 65 IPC Magazines/Robert Harding Syndication, 67 Jane Churchill, 68(tr)David Parmiter, 68(c,b) Eaglemoss Publications/Steve Tanner, 69(bl) Rufflette, 69(br) Eaglemoss Publications/Graham Rae, 70(t,b) Eaglemoss Publications/Tif Hunter/Graham Rae, 70(c) Rufflette, 71 David Downie, 72 Rufflette, 73, 74, Eaglemoss Publications/Simon Page-Ritchie, 75 Design Archives, 76 IPC Magazines/Robert Harding Syndication, 77 Textra, 78 Swish, 79, 80 Eaglemoss Publications/Tif Hunter, 85 IPC Magazines/Robert Harding Syndication, 86(tr) Romo Ltd, 86(bl) Eaglemoss Publications/Graham Rae, 87 Anna French, 88 Jane Churchill, 89(tr) IPC Magazines/Robert Harding Syndication, 89(br) Jane Churchill, 90, 91 IPC Magazines/Robert Harding Syndication, 92 EWA/Tommy Candler, 93 Cy de Cosse, 94 Eaglemoss Publications/Iain Bagwell, 95 IPC Magazines/Robert Harding Syndication, 97, 98 Osborne & Little, 99 Sanderson, 100 Ariadne Holland, 101-105 IPC Magazines/Robert Harding Syndication, 106 Eaglemoss Publications/Simon Page-Ritchie, 107-118 Eaglemoss Publications/Graham Rae, 119-122 Eaglemoss Publications/Mark Wood, 123-125 IPC Magazines/Robert Harding Syndication, 126 Sanderson.

Illustrations

8-10 John Hutchinson, 12 Aziz Kahn, 14 Terry Evans, 16-22 John Hutchinson, 23, 24 Terry Evans, 26-28, John Hutchinson, 29-32 Terry Evans, 34-72 John Hutchinson, 73, 74 Terry Evans, 77, 78 John Hutchinson, 79-84 Terry Evans, 86-92 John Hutchinson, 94 Terry Evans, 96-106 John Hutchinson, 107, 108 Terry Evans, 110-112 John Hutchinson, 113, 114 Terry Evans, 116-126 John Hutchinson.